A Grieving Mother's Guide to Running Away In Mexico

Nina Poznekoff

ISBN: 978-0-9948670-0-1

Front and back cover formatted by Nina Poznekoff

Typeset in *Walbaum* at SpicaBookDesign

Printed and bound in Canada
by Printorium Bookworks / Island Blue,
Victoria, B.C.

To my son, Steve

You should still be here…

Day 1

Six months have passed since the unthinkable happened. Six months have passed since I heard the shocking news my son had left this earth.

If you wonder what the last six months have been like for me, you would have to ask others for I know not what I was doing; I know not what I was saying. I only know I was waiting.

I was waiting for God or the universe or whoever has a semblance of control over us lowly humans to wake up from their sleep. I was waiting for them to say no mother could live through the loss of her child, so they had only been napping. God had been napping and missed the occurrence of my son's death, so now that He was awake, surely He would give my son back to me. Surely He wouldn't leave me alone on this earth when all I had was my child. Surely this wasn't happening and I was imagining it.

So I sat, holding my breath, for six months, waiting for the unthinkable, the unimaginable, the sorrow of all sorrows to just be a cruel joke played on me. I sat waiting, wondering when my son would call. I knew it had to be a mistake. It just had to be.

Slowly, I began to exhale.

And with each breath I took on this earth where I was no longer a mom, no longer needed, no longer a part of someone, no longer alive, no longer a rational human being, no longer a functioning member of society, the searing pain tore through me like a brush fire.

The pain, the pain, the pain.

The torture of the all encompassing pain.

I didn't know what to do...

So, I went to Mexico.

Just Kelly, the dog my son left me, and I flew to a fishing village somewhere in Mexico.

The plane was full of party revelers because most travelers were headed to their vacation destination and the mood was high. All but for one...

Sitting beside me were a young couple who had left their three children with grandma and the young mother spoke longingly for her children even though she had only left them that morning, and would see them again in less than two weeks.

I said all the right words, nodded at all the right times, while my heart was screaming at her to stop talking. The more tequilas her husband drank, the more amorous he became with his young wife, and I envied them their innocence in life.

Finally, the question came. An innocent, innocuous question asked by many throughout the years. "Do you have children?"

I told her I didn't know how to answer and that my child had died.

Instantly I saw the shock and then came the moment where you could see her struggle with what to say next.

There was nothing to say.

And I wondered how this had become my life?

And I wondered how long I would have to stay behind?

And I pleaded to a God I no longer trusted to be merciful and take me to be with my son.

And I waited for Day 2 in Mexico knowing nothing could bring me joy.

And I wanted the earth to swallow me up.

Day 2

Kelly the dog and I were very tired and slept soundly in our new surroundings. The crowing of the roosters awakened us, followed by the loud music of a passing truck. In this part of Mexico it would appear shocks on a vehicle are unheard of and the bounce of the passing motorist on the cobblestone roads was a sound which could not be ignored.

Still jetlagged, I momentarily forgot where I was. Looking around the unfamiliar room brought me to a resounding jolt and I quickly remembered that Kelly the dog was an unwilling participant in what seemed to me to be a good idea at the time.

It's strange to see the new person I'm becoming unfold and many times my actions and my words are a surprise. I now refer to myself as the "old me" and the "new and unimproved me".

The "old me" would have had all her travel itinerary meticulously organized, along with her packing and her knowledge of her surroundings.

This "new me" was quite astounded to find, upon opening the suitcase, that she'd forgotten to pack enough clothes. There appeared to be many socks, but few shirts and shorts. I would have enough toothpaste to last a few years, and yet no thought was given to much else.

It was as if I didn't care.

I didn't.

I plodded one foot in front of the other and proceeded on with my day. Every day that passes is one more day without my son, and I find these days a personal insult. How dare you continue, world? How dare you still shine, sun? How dare you laugh, people? How dare you taunt me by still finding joy, peace, laughter, happiness, hope in this world that could take my only child? How dare you?

And yet, while my heart would like to shrivel up and die, my head knows there are still things that need to be done. Many times I resent having to look after Kelly the dog because if I didn't, then maybe I wouldn't have to move, think, feel, get dressed, go outside, or do any of the nonsensical things others take for granted, and yet to me, are now so arduous.

No matter what my thoughts and feelings, Kelly the dog still needed to pee.

Off we went.

The small sidewalks were littered with garbage and the tiny, clapboard houses were open to the eyes of any passerby. I saw cement floors painted a myriad of colors and in one corner would be the bed, while alongside would sit the dining room table with a large candelabra hanging overhead. It didn't appear to fit and yet it all fit in these new, eclectic surroundings I'd found myself in.

Kelly the dog walked alongside me and wasn't going to venture far. Within seconds we heard the barking of many dogs and she quickly glued herself to my leg and was going no further, full bladder or not.

Kelly the dog was smart enough to feel trepidation.

I was not.

Soon some of the barking dogs came up to her. It was quickly evident these dogs were malnourished and while most were content to sniff Kelly and walk away, some looked as though they thought she might be quite delicious.

We rapidly backed away and headed a different direction.

I met the landlady and her husband and they seemed very nice. The landlady knew what happened to my son and said Kelly the dog appeared to be very sad. You could tell they wanted to be friendly, but it was too much effort for me. It is all so tiring to make new acquaintances and learn their life story. The "old me" would have had a wonderful time getting to know these people. The "new me" just wants to avoid everyone. And yet, when I avoid everyone, I am very lonely. My family is gone, my child was my world and now I feel adrift and lost in a world I no longer see as warm or inviting.

The loneliness is palpable.

And I wonder if this is how my son felt?

After breakfast Kelly the dog and I made our way to the beach. This is a fisherman's beach and there was not a lot to observe except for fishing boats and pelicans.

Kelly jumped into the ocean waves, chasing a stick I threw for her. Taking off my runners and socks I let the warm sand squish between my toes and felt the salty water lap against my legs. Someone watching would have thought, "What a peaceful, happy scene."

I watched the palms trees sway in a light breeze and somewhere heard the laughter of a child. The tears came and would not stop. Try as I might to control, they poured from my eyes.

A few short months ago the beauty I had encountered would have made my heart sing. Now, there were only tears. There was no joy. There was no awe at God's handiwork. There was only pain. There was nothing that could soothe, nothing that could quell this grief. Nothing. There's nothing to ease the pain. There's no words to describe what I feel because these words haven't been invented yet. Why haven't they been invented? Because no one should feel what I'm feeling. No one should have to wonder what words can describe this pain.

Kelly the dog and I went back to our new home.

We will try again tomorrow.

Day 3

Day 3 in an endless amount of days left without my son. How will I go on when I so much don't want to? What will make me want to go on when my reason for living is gone? Why would I even want to try?

I woke up this morning at 6 a.m to the sound of a loudspeaker blaring outside my window. Since the owner of the megaphone was speaking Spanish, I'm sure he was selling coca cola, for those were the only words I could make out. Others have since told me he was selling propane. No matter. At that hour of the morning, who needs either?

Kelly the dog and I will be changing our sleeping time and whereas, back in Canada, midnight was mid evening for me, now it will have to be a time of sleep.

It's lonely in Mexico. It's lonely in Canada. It's also lonely in my heart and even though I say that it was ripped out when I heard of my son's passing, it must still beat inside me, and it must still be able to feel. This heart no longer feels joy; it only feels sorrow and pain. This heart is no longer necessary and would be better to stop beating altogether.

I sometimes wish I had the courage to end my life. But, I'm too afraid, so I exist semi-alive, semi-dead, with no hope for a brighter future.

When others tell me that time will heal and someday I will find great joy again, I feel angry. While my head understands everyone is just trying to do the best they can and help me in any way they can, my heart wishes, just for a moment, that they could experience the loss of a child, and see how long it will take them to "find great joy" again.

I truly believed that, in this life, my son and I would win against incredible odds. It was what kept me fighting and struggling so hard for a better life for him and I. But, we lost. We both lost. Don't tell me I'm still here so it means there is still hope for me. There is no hope for me. My child is gone. What could ever make it ok? What could ever have any meaning or purpose again? Some people, when they experience a loss as great as this, go on and help others. I don't want to. I've endeavoured to be kind and caring and loving and unselfish my entire life. And this was my thank you. And now I no longer want to be any of those things. I just want to curl in a corner and have life pass me by. I just want to wait it out until death takes me. I just want to be with my son.

So, why do I plod one foot in front of the other looking for a semblance of peace? It is because I'm too afraid to do anything else.

Today is Thursday and market day in the small town of La Penita. It is the day to buy all your fruits and vegetables and as I'd been existing on restaurant meals these past two days, it was time to stock up and homestead in my tiny apartment.

I walked the hot, cobblestone side street where many Mexican people had laid out their wares. It was a necessary venture and within a few hours I'd seen all I wanted to see and bought all I wanted to buy.

Returning to the apartment I found Kelly the dog excited to see me and she barked her welcome. Many times I look at her and think, "It's almost as if you were given a job to do; a job to look after me, and you're taking your responsibility seriously." For, right now, Kelly the dog is my only companion in what could be a great adventure, or what just could be a continuation of my existence. I know the choice is mine, and where many times before, I chose the positive, now I know I choose the negative. I make no apologies for it and feel no need to explain.

My landlady had invited me over to meet a friend who was also from Canada. This lady had moved to Mexico many years before and was about my age; also single, and very pleasant. Now I find idle conversation so incredibly difficult and am still perplexed and confused by this new person I've become. The "old me", who lived in the same world her son lived in, would have befriended this woman and made plans to get together at a later date. This "new and unimproved me" made no such overtures and left shortly after having a polite conversation with this woman.

This is a lonely journey.

I thought I came to Mexico to be alone and grieve my son.

I'm not sure I know how.

Kelly the dog and I took a walk to the beach before dinner. Yesterday I had seen a snake at the water's edge and its head was burrowed in the sand. As the tide would rush in, it covered the snake, but as it would recede, I could see the snake writhing and wiggling its way deeper into the sand. I asked the landlady about it and she said in all the years she's lived here, she's never seen a water snake, but yes, they do exist and are actually quite poisonous. She said I must not be a very lucky person to see a snake so soon after arriving.

Yes, I agreed. I no longer felt like a very lucky person.

Returning for our second time to this beach, Kelly and I were very watchful as to where we treaded. Dogs run wild and free here and while we were at the beach, three dogs started barking and running towards Kelly. As I've mentioned before, Kelly looks very well fed, while these dogs look as though they are starving.

I was afraid for Kelly, and Kelly was hiding behind me. I do sometimes question her "pit bull" status.

The owner of the dogs' assured me they were fine and as I sat on a log watching the ocean waves, he proceeded to tell me his life story in surprisingly well spoken English. He said he and his wife lived in California, but his mother lived here in Mexico so he came down often to look after her. He spoke lovingly of his mother and I told him it was good that he looked after her so well; to which he responded that you only have one mother, whereas wives, they come and go. I thought that was an interesting concept, but find idle conversation tiring, so got up to leave. He shook my hand and wished me well in Mexico.

I, too, wish me well in Mexico...

Day 4

This morning started early with my 6 a.m. wake up call from the megaphone packing truck driver. I'm still sure he's selling coca cola, but it could be my limited knowledge of Spanish. I have now deduced this will be a regular morning occurrence and am trying my utmost to change my sleep cycle to accommodate his schedule.

In this new world I've been thrown into, his daily morning routine of bellowing his business has almost given me a false comfort of familiarity. It would appear we humans are creatures of habit and I've already embraced the morning ritual of being loudly awoken to the sound of his voice.

Today I feel very tired and sad. I don't know what to do here. My thoughts of walking my dog long distances were quickly squelched as it is too hot to walk anywhere during the day. In the night I venture nowhere other than just outside the locked front gate so Kelly the dog can have her nightly pee. And any exploration we attempted was met with aforementioned packs of hungry dogs. If Kelly could speak, I'm sure she would say, "You go on without me. I'm fine sitting here in the apartment waiting for you." So far, it would appear Kelly the dog is not overly impressed with Mexico, and I am starting to think, not overly impressed with me.

Who can blame her?

I'm not overly impressed with me either...

Yesterday my landlady told me about a place where I can buy coffee grounds to make coffee in my apartment. Kelly and I ventured over in search of said coffee place and as we passed over a small bridge, there appeared many dogs on the rooftops of the clapboard houses and they looked mad and mean. Kelly and I quickly retreated and today I will go by myself to buy the coffee.

I don't really understand why I talk so much about the danger Kelly is in. I think it's maybe because she is my only link to anything familiar and while I don't fear for me at all, I do fear for her. I think losing her would be my final undoing, not that I'm not already undone.

I ventured out in search of my daily need for sustenance; the ever welcome morning cup of coffee. Upon arriving at my destination, the purchase of coffee was successfully completed. Now to the more difficult task of explaining coffee filters to the Mexican senora. Many hand gestures later she finally produced the filters. On the package was a list price of 20 pesos ($2.00 American) but after much deliberation with her amiga (friend), it was decided that the new price, for me and me only, was going to be 30 pesos ($3.00). More hand gestures followed, although I held back on the one I really wanted to use, and the senora remained firm that they had written the wrong price on the package of coffee filters. It would appear that 20 pesos was only a suggestion, and could be changed depending on her whim.

I had two choices: pay the new and unimproved price or take my business elsewhere.

Feeling frustrated that I was at the mercy of this unscrupulous store vendor, I decided to take my business elsewhere. Many gruelling, heat filled footsteps later, after checking in store after store, I returned to this same senora and paid the price of 30 pesos. The only positive thing to this experience was I now knew how to ask for filtre para cafe which means coffee filter in Spanish.

A lesson learned.

The old me would have brushed this off and even retold the story laughingly. This new me was not amused.

The rest of the day passed uneventfully and I spent time in the apartment watching Spanish television. Frustrated with wasting my time in that way, I finally donned my bathing suit, grabbed a towel, book, and Kelly and headed to the rooftop to suntan. Within moments of the hot sun beating on my body, I went in search of the small swimming pool to the back of the property. Aaah, heaven! The swimming pool had been built out of part of their garage and had no sun access to it at all. Quickly my body temperature cooled down and I was ready to pursue my continued quest for a smokin' tan.

All around is paradise and yet there is no rest in my soul. The old me had always said that peace and paradise exist within oneself and searching the world for it will never bring you satisfaction. The old me had a son.

This one only has the memories...

Day 5

I've decided I don't want to sit at my computer and write a daily journal. I don't want to, but I must, for it is only in writing that my true feelings come out. Otherwise, I am now a jumble of emotions who don't know what to be from moment to moment, and who can also change from moment to moment.

The old me was a person of extremes. There was very little grey in my life and most things were either black or white. The abusive childhood I survived became an abusive adulthood, which I also survived. Because I had known so much cruelty at the hands and words of the very people I should have been able to trust, the best way I knew to survive was to live life to the fullest. I'd heard it said many times through my growing up years that the best revenge was to live a good life.

So, I tried.

I tried so hard.

And when I cried, my very soul shed tears of pain.

And when I laughed, I could feel my entire body vibrate with the joy.

And when I loved, I loved fully and deeply.

And when I hurt, I chose to never feel hatred for the ones who hurt me.

Those were my survival instincts and, for me, they seemed to work.

They seemed to.

Until now...

Now I have no survival instincts and I second guess every decision I made as a mother. I second guess every decision I made as a human being and feel as though I am on trial in a court of law where I am defendant, prosecutor, judge and jury.

How do you plead?

Guilty, your honour!

Guilty of never being there enough for my son, guilty of never allowing him to make mistakes but constantly pushing him to be better, stronger, kinder, wiser, worth loving, worth living, worth something.

Guilty, your honour!

Guilty of putting others needs before his, guilty of pushing him aside when I didn't know how to respond, guilty of a cruel tongue when I was tired or stressed or overworked or overwhelmed.

Guilty, your honour!

Guilty of not being there for him as he reached out to me, guilty for being 3000 miles away from him in Arizona as he said "Mom, please call me back. It's very important." Those were the last words I would ever hear my son say, for shortly thereafter they say he took his own life.

Guilty, your honour!

I was his mother, we were each other's best friends, we were all we had, why wasn't I there to care?

Guilty, your honour!

I've heard all the evidence and am ready to pass sentence.

Guilty, you are.

The only reasonable punishment is to make you walk this earth knowing you could have helped your son and didn't. You are guilty of his death and the worst punishment you can now experience is to spend every waking second with this guilt on your shoulders.

I accept, your honour, for guilty I am.

Today I was awakened to the harmonious sound of

my morning megaphone man selling his wares. I still say he's screaming out coca-cola, but need to confess that, as I looked out onto the street below, he had a truck load of what looked to be propane tanks. I'm sure before I leave here, I will properly distinguish what he is trying to say and just as I learned how to say coffee filter in Spanish, so will I know how to say propane tank. Until then, coca-cola it is and coca-cola it will stay.

Even after only five short days, his voice now had a familiar sound to it and once I was reassured he was out doing what needed to be done, I was able to roll over and go back to sleep. Kelly the dog was peacefully sleeping on the floor beside me, but once she'd notice I'd awoken, she'd jump up on the bed and cuddle beside me. Somehow she makes it not so lonely and burrows in deep so I have no choice but to put my arms around her and hug. The hugging seems to release some need inside me and I truly don't believe that we, as humans, were meant to live alone.

I took my time getting ready this morning and slowly sipped the coffee purchased yesterday. It was the best coffee I'd ever had and I know I will be returning to the unscrupulous senora for more. I know when I'm licked.

While breakfast was making I decided to take Kelly for her morning routine. Yesterday I overheard my landlord telling someone that my perro was bueno. That means my dog was good. It made me feel good to hear that and now, instead of calling her Kelly, I call her Bueno Perro. She seems to understand.

As I need to buy a few vegetables for my supper tonight, Kelly and I walk to the village square, which is about 8 city blocks from where I live. Once we walk the 8 blocks, we then come to what can best be described as a Mexican freeway. There is a streetlight of sorts to cross this busy intersection, but once again, it appears that things here are merely a suggestion and not a rule. When the light turns green, you go for all you've got because some motorists stop and some don't. I've taught Kelly to "run, Perro, run" and run she does.

In this part of Mexico, pedestrians don't have the right of way and the motorists go where they please. Today, as I was crossing a side street, a delivery truck was backing up and nudged me slightly before stepping on the brakes. I do confess to never paying attention anymore and know I need to be more watchful. As I walked past the truck, the driver yelled "sorry" to me, and I thought, "why?"

It would have been ok, it really would have.

As I meandered, unnoticed, through the busy main street, the noise seemed to permeate my soul. Everyone was yelling at everyone else. I have jokingly decided Mexican people are slightly deaf, for everything is said loudly and expressively. Music blares from every shop owner's store, children are crying, laughing, running, dogs are barking, whining, sniffing; the noise and commotion and exuberance is contagious and I can feel my inner soul want to join in. I want to escape into the noise and commotion and camraderie and adventure and excitement, but my heart feels encased in cement. My heart, my will, my choice, my pain, my grief won't let me, and I feel like the only person not invited to a party.

So I walk to the ocean where Kelly and I can be alone.

This is the third time I've been at the ocean and each time I cry. I have decided now that this portion of the Pacific Ocean, while beautiful, has become my crying ocean. It is where the tears flow and where I let them. Sometimes the pain is too much to bear and I try to hold them in. Sometimes I succeed, sometimes I don't.

An elderly fisherman approached me and spoke in rapid Spanish. While I'm blond haired and fair skinned, most Mexican people speak to me in long Spanish sentences and don't seem to hear me when I say "non comprendre" which means "I don't understand."

I smiled politely and continued on my sojourn. Since seeing the water snake on the first day, I no longer wade at the tide's edge and keep my head down, watchful for anything that might poke its head from the sand. Even though I now feel no fear for my life, apparently my deadly fear of snakes has not abated.

My perro and I walked past a group of playing children and as they noticed Kelly they enthusiastically ran up to her and wanted to play. We fetched a stick for Kelly and the children took turns throwing it far into the ocean waves. Kelly has yet to understand the ocean and seemed almost surprised as the waves slapped her on the backside and propelled her toward the sandy beach. When thirsty, she would lap at the salty water and then turn away in seeming distaste.

My heart was heavy watching the playful scene on this beautiful summer day and I needed to walk away. Kelly and I left the playing children still clamoring for one more throw of the stick, but I said my adios (goodbye) and left.

We continued on our morning walk to nowhere, my Bueno Perro and me...

At some point, we reached rock bluffs and I did an about face, all the while feeling the unshed tears bubbling and desperately clawing their way to the surface. I pushed them back for I wanted a day without crying, but the tears were stronger. They won out just at the moment I again reached the gaggle of playful children Kelly and I had left an hour before.

The children ran towards my Perro and wanted to throw the stick for her again. Not wanting them to see me cry, the tears receded like an ocean wave, as quickly as they had come. I smiled and watched as they and Kelly enjoyed the day.

Why wasn't my son here to enjoy it with them?

The rest of the day was spent tanning on the rooftop, cooking and eating my supper and watching a Spanish movie.

While Kelly the dog is great company, I'm feeling a bit lonely for human interaction. I still don't want to engage in conversation with anyone, but it would just be nice to be around others. This morning I passed a quaint little karaoke bar and am now deciding whether to go or not. I was always the type of person who wouldn't even go to a restaurant by herself. Everything was so much better when you had someone else to share it with. But, now I have no choice. Well, actually I have two choices. I can stay in this apartment alone with my perro or I can venture out alone.

I did neither. I ventured out with Kelly and listened to the noise of the village square.

I miss my son.

We both deserved so much better than we got...

Day 6

When I go outside, I feel alive; when I sit and hide, I feel the pain.

Going out is such an effort and all seems so painstakingly difficult to do. Decisions that were once made without thought are now arduous and difficult to make. What to wear, what to eat, what to do, what to say, what does it matter? Now, none of it matters, and yet some small part of me still wants it to.

Directly overhead my laptop computer is a mirror and when I quickly look up I see a woman who once was pretty. What good does being pretty do you when you have no luck? Would be better to be homely and lucky. Actually would be better to be both, but we shouldn't want too much in life.

Or should we? I always felt as though I was making some unspoken deal with God. If you will just look after my son and keep him safe, then I'll rarely complain and be happy with my lot in life. If only he can remain safe in this world, then I'm ok with living without. It was ok that I never had a happy marriage, but a short lived, unhappy one. It was ok that I lived in a tiny house with few nice things. It was ok that my furniture didn't match and my tea towels were old. It was all ok, God, except for one thing. Just keep my child safe. I didn't want much out of this world and couldn't even keep the one thing I'd asked for.

I'd watch others complain about the smallest detail and then was quite astounded that nothing bigger would come their way to stop the whining about nothing. It would appear that somehow they had a magic solution to life where they would complain about everything and then maybe God or whoever were too afraid to make them unhappy so it was made sure nothing more happened to them. People would always say that who knew what the future held for them, maybe there would be some disaster around the corner. I never wanted to think anyone was a sitting duck waiting for disaster to strike, but just in case, I was going to make sure I didn't make the big guy upstairs mad about anything. I was going to make sure and not demand much out of this life and work hard and try hard and be honest and be grateful and be kind and be caring and be loving. And I decided long ago to not feel hatred towards anyone. Goodness knows, I had justifiable reason for some were very cruel, but I taught my child and I taught myself to always forgive; never hold a grudge; never wish ill to others. I apparently taught us wrong. For in doing that, did I somehow teach my child that his wishes weren't as important as others? Did I somehow teach him that he couldn't make a mistake and still be loved? Did I somehow teach him it was up to him to succeed in life and if he didn't, he was to blame?

I think I did.

I talked to his friends and they said he was the type who couldn't fail. While many of them, now in their thirties, returned home to their parents after losing their jobs or girlfriends or wives or whatever disaster seemed to befall them, my son wouldn't have allowed his pride to let him come home. He would have had to make a success of his life and if not, then he would die trying. And die he did.

Dear God. Not death...

Let him be angry or avoid me or lose his home or lose his fight, or lose whatever it is he had to hang on to so tightly. Let him move away and not communicate for a long time until he found his way again. Let him come home and live with me even though he was thirty three years old and would have felt a failure. Let him be a failure.

But, not death, God...

Not death...

Be merciful to me and take me, too. Please God.

Today my trusty perro and I walked to the nearest town called Rincon De Guayabitos. It was a long and grueling walk there; about 2 ½ miles, and we walked over a swinging suspension bridge that was precarious to say the least. I said "mi dios" (my god) more than once as we swung with the wind and I know Kelly the dog concurred.

La Penita, where I live, is definitely the working poor and there are few niceties here. Rincon de Guayabitos is a tourist town and you quickly notice the poor don't live there. Upon crossing the suspension bridge, I was instantly thrown into a world of even pavement, beautiful homes, unbroken sidewalks and streets lined with bougainvillea plants that were a delight to the eye. The rich purples, deep pinks and vibrant orange blossoms rose majestically towards the heavens and you felt drawn to smell the beautiful flowers. It always surprised me that God would give no scent to something so beautiful. Not that I would dare tell God what to do, but couldn't He have made them smell like something? Oranges? Strawberries? Anything? But, no, as you bend to take a branch in your hand and bring it towards your nose, no scent awaits you.

Before, it didn't matter. I relished the beauty of the plant. Now, everything matters. And nothing makes sense. And nothing is as it should be. And now, it bugs me. But, who am I?

The perro and I were hot and tired after our long walk so stopped at an outdoor restaurant with a view of the ocean. This was truly paradise and everyone seemed to be enjoying themselves. I was glad I hadn't chosen Rincon de Guayabitos to live in because the laughter and happiness disturbed me and made me want to cry. Was it really only a few short months ago that my laughter would have been the loudest and happiest on the beach? Only a few short months ago and the happiness inside was dead, along with my child.

We ate quickly and decided to walk along the beach on our way home. I thought I'll figure it out as we go and somehow end up back in La Penita. Since I'd seen the water snake on my first day here, I'd been very nervous sticking my toes in the murky ocean water, but while in Rincon, decided that just for today I'm not going to let my fear of snakes stop me from enjoying the waves. So, I walked the entire two miles with the sand sucking my toes and the water cooling me off, my faithful perro beside me.

Every few hundred yards, we'd stop so I could throw Kelly a stick and many would laugh as they'd watch her search for the ever elusive stick in the rushing ocean waves. She would search the water over until she found her prize and come out of the water victorious in her quest. What a good dog she is. Truly a Bueno Perro.

As it was low tide, we were able to climb some rock bluffs and cross the shallow water to get to the beach in La Penita, so walked back a different way than we had come. It appeared my inner self knew I was back at my crying ocean for as I walked, I sobbed. I sobbed loudly this time and even though life in La Penita is very lonely, I know this is the reason I came. I need to see if there can ever be a purpose for my life to go on. I need to see if this grief will ever subside even a miniscule amount so I can find a reason for being. I need to decide if I will continue to plod one foot after another because, right now, I so desperately don't want to. I know some friends are worried I came here to end my life, but that is not my purpose for being here. That is only my desire.

I ran the race of life and lost. My son and I, we lost. Life beat us down and two people died with one bullet. I am the walking dead. Will I ever feel alive again? At this point, I don't want to.

Walking on the beach in La Penita I saw my second snake sunning itself. My landlady would think I was truly unlucky now, and I would agree.

Then I wondered, as this is all I now seem to fear, do I keep seeing these snakes so I realize I now need fear nothing; nothing at all?

I don't know.

It doesn't matter.

Day 7

Today I feel restless and don't want to write. I slept fitfully and dreamt about my son as a little boy. In the dream I hugged him and it seemed like such a motherly thing to do. Something I no longer am is a mother; it was something I used to be. I can't rationalize this new concept and I can't wrap my head around the fact that I failed as a mother. For, if I did the best I could, and if my child is dead by his own hand, then the best I could wasn't very good, was it? I failed him in so many ways. I couldn't protect him from all the family abuse. I couldn't, wouldn't or didn't protect him when my brothers were cruel and hateful. I didn't protect him from the angry words hurled at him by unkind people. I didn't protect him from us being beaten by my mother and her two sisters when he was only four years old. I didn't protect him from my faults as a mother. I didn't know how.

After years of seeing my child hurt, I turned off somehow. I thought that as long as we pretended everything was alright, then it would be so. When he would try and talk to me about painful things, I would push him away because I couldn't bear his pain. I would make jokes or make light of his need to talk to me and never let him get as close as he tried to be.

It hurt too much to love him.

It hurt too much to need him.

It hurt too much to watch him hurt.

So, I pretended it all wasn't happening.

I would see the frustration in his eyes and I would turn away.

It hurt too much to see him hurt.

I questioned how a child could heal from all we'd lived

through. I questioned how he could ever be whole. Many times we reminded each other of our painful lives and I know sometimes he avoided me as much as I avoided him.

When he was in his early twenties, he came home to visit and sat me down for what he called "the first adult conversation we ever had." He questioned me on why we had to move so many times and I was truthful with him for the first time ever. I told him we had to run for our lives because my mother was mentally ill and would hear voices telling her to do us harm. I told him we had to run for our lives because she would hire people to kidnap him and harm me and my family was very rich so money was no object. I told him I was so sorry for the terrible life he'd led, and I cried the entire time I spoke. He looked pained, but told me to set myself free and not hold in the pain, for even though it was a sad childhood, he turned out pretty great, and even though we lived without and lived very poorly, he always knew I loved him.

I did.

And I do.

And I can't bear that he's no longer with me.

I can't bear this pain.

I'm sitting alone in Mexico, missing my baby, wanting him near. I'm sitting alone in Mexico and the tears won't subside. I'm sitting alone in Mexico, more alone than I've ever been.

So, today, I hate. I've never allowed myself to hate before so this is a foreign feeling to me. I understand now why I didn't hate because it is an overpowering, self-destructive, helpless feeling.

But, now I hate.

I hate all those who hurt my son and mostly I hate my brothers. I hate them for never being there for us in all the years of abuse and all the years we ran away to hide from the abuse. I hate them for being able to raise their children without fear. I hate them for their cruelty to me, but mostly for their cruelty to my son. I hate them for being cowards and taking the easy, comfortable way out. I hate them for keeping all the family money and family property, while my son and I struggled to survive. I hate them for never showing love to their nephew. I hate them for leaving us all alone. I hate them for doing so much harm to us and once we no longer tried to get close to them, telling people that it was our choice to not be close. I hate them for lying about us. I hate them for saying things that weren't true and weren't kind. I hate them for never hugging my child. I hate them.

I hate...

I hate...

I hate...

But who I hate most of all...

Is me.

For I failed my child.

And now my child is gone.

This morning in La Penita, I struggled to awaken. I wanted to exist in the dreamworld where I was hugging my young son, but couldn't.

The maid was knocking at the door and I reluctantly brought myself back to this world, the real world where I live without my child. Quickly I got dressed, but when I opened the door, she was already gone. Thinking maybe I'd dreamt she was there, I went back to the safety of my bed, only to be awoken by another loud knock.

Throwing a shirt over my nightgown, I ran for the door and there was Pete, my friend from Canada. His wife, Heidi, had been ill for the past few days, but now asked if I would like to come to their house on the outskirts of La Penita. I had never been to the house they were building and excitedly got ready to go. I know I am missing human contact and while I love Kelly, sometimes I need someone who talks back.

They showed me their house and it was fabulous. Pete was a bricklayer by trade and built the entire four story home with the top floor an open patio with a view to take your breath away.

Heidi and I sat upstairs while Pete played with Kelly and today I broke down. She held me and hugged me while I sat and cried for my son. Their son had died some years back and our two boys had gone to high school together. A mutual friend of our sons had introduced us as we were both mothers in grief. I love my new friends, but hate the reason we had to meet.

I tire easily now and find I run out of things to say. When I have an especially emotional day where the tears just flow, I get disoriented and can't make sense out of things. I feel lost, wander aimlessly, and speak without thought. This is so different from the person I used to be who was known for her sense of humor and contagious laughter. This is not the woman I want to be.

But, I would be her or anyone else if only my child were still alive.

Was I too selfish a mother?

Did I think of me first and my child last?

Did I not meet his needs enough?

Will I question for the rest of my days?

I believe I will, and will always be found wanting.

Then, I want the rest of my days to be short.

This is a sad day, and no amount of sunshine, no amount of warmth, no amount of beauty, has made its way into my heart.

Day 8

After only seven short days here I am starting to settle in and belong; well, as much as I belong anywhere in this strange world I've been thrown into.

Today I'd thought to spend the day suntanning and lying by the pool, so quickly breakfasted and went outside to take the dog for her morning ritual. As I walked out of the gated complex, someone in a van honked their horn. Since horns are constantly honking here, along with roosters crowing, dogs barking, people talking, I paid no heed.

Soon the van pulled to the curb and someone yelled my name. It was the woman I had been introduced to by my landlady. Her name is Doris and she moved here from Canada years ago. She recently bought a house in Bucerias, which is a town about an hour's drive.

It warmed me to have someone notice me on the busy street. There was a feeling of camraderie and kinship and I didn't feel quite so alone.

We talked and made tentative plans for me to take the bus to Bucerias and maybe meet for dinner one night. The old me would have been excited at the prospect of this venture while this new me wondered if she could keep the conversation flowing without breaking down in tears. I'd already learnt others are uncomfortable with my tears so hold them in. For me, it is a conundrum. If I let my grief show, then I am alone. If I hold it in, then people draw to me, but I feel emptier and sadder.

I think it is good I am in Mexico. When the grief overwhelms, I have no agenda. That, in itself, sometimes makes me feel so alone. But I came here to grieve my son, to see if I could continue to live without him, and to find a reason to go on. Maybe I've got too big a wish list, but if even one of those things is accomplished, I will be the better for it.

As I rounded the corner to our building, dog in tow, my landlord was outside doing some work and, in halting English, told me new tenants had moved in and did I want to meet them? I didn't, but politeness always wins out, so said I would. His wife took me to meet the elderly couple, also from Canada, and we made idle chitchat for a few moments before I excused myself and left.

I was quite enjoying the solitude of living in this apartment complex by myself, and whereas before would have thought the more the merrier, now am not looking forward to the many people moving in. My landlady, in thinking she was saying something good, told me that when everyone arrives, there will be potlucks and parties and get togethers and outings. I wonder if she noticed the grimace on my face as she was expounding the virtues of the arrival of others.

After meeting the new couple, I passed by the pool and noticed my landlord and his helper scraping and painting the wall directly beside the pool. This pool would not be operational until the work was done.

On to plan B. If only I had a plan B...

When all else fails, I go to my crying ocean and walk beside the waves. Sighting not one, but two snakes since my arrival keeps me watchful and on guard for what I'm sure will soon be snake number three.

This morning the fishermen were busy preparing their small fishing boats for the catches to be made during the day. Some had already gone out and were back cleaning their catch on the sandy shore.

At one point, Kelly and I walked by just as the fishermen had finished cleaning and you saw massive amounts of egrets and pelicans waiting for the spoils. Kelly and I continued to walk when suddenly there was loud screeching and the birds swooped down towards the beach, mere inches from my head. While I was very aware of their presence, they were oblivious to me and were intent on their prey.

It was something out of a Stephen King movie and while I've taken no pictures because the raw beauty of this area is a personal affront to me, at this moment, I wished I had my camera. There were literally hundreds of the gigantic birds swooping and diving, diving and squawking.

Kelly and I continued on our way. The rest of the beach was deserted save for an older gentleman lying at the water's edge apparently taking a bath. As we passed by, he hobbled to a corner of the beach where I noticed his outer clothing and a cane. Painstakingly, he raised himself on his cane and sauntered away.

Kelly and I continued to walk, stopping every so often to throw the elusive stick into the ocean waves.

Kelly has learned to circumvent the high waves and now knows that if she waits long enough, eventually the stick will make its way to her. She is a smart bueno perro.

Sitting at my crying ocean, I felt the tears come to the surface and let them come. They do not heal, they do not soothe, they do not stop. Why am I here?

How is it this is my life?

A life without my son...

Day 9

I don't know what to say today. It was a surreal kind of day with many emotional twists and turns and I want to convey my true feelings, but feel so hindered and crippled in my thoughts, my words, and my actions.

Outwardly I appear to have a semblance of intelligence and present well to the world. But inside I'm a turmoil of emotions and now find my actions are more a reaction than a well thought out process. It is only after the fact that I realize no thought, no caring, no planning goes into anything I do. I seem to present a dichotomy between thought and action, and it's only by sheer luck that nothing worse has happened to me.

Although I almost want to smirk at the idea that anything worse than losing my son could happen to me. There is nothing worse.

I woke up plagued with a turmoil of emotions. There was agitation, anger, despair, grief, sorrow, remorse, guilt, sadness, shame, despondency, and I questioned the purpose of this day, like I question the purpose of any day since my son is gone.

I questioned the purpose of God in our lives and wondered where He now fit in. Growing up I didn't have a concept of God. He was just somewhere up in the sky looking down but really didn't have a lot to do with my life.

Then, when my marriage ended and I was left alone with a newborn son, I thought there had to be more to life than life and began to search for God. What I found answered all my unanswered questions and filled me with a purpose for being. What I thought I found made sense of all the wrong done to my son and me, and when the world was cruel and unjust, I looked to God to be kind and just.

I struggled somewhat with the concept of an almighty God and credit that to the old adage that you tend to view God as you view your earthly father. My earthly father was a kind man with sparkly blue eyes who had a heart full of love, but he was always overpowered by the cruel and hateful person that was my mother. To me, God was like my dad; kind, loving, giving, unselfish, but lacked power over evil. Also to me, the devil was like my mother; cruel, hateful, a liar, selfish, evil, abusive, but with much power. For, you see, she won in life. Life never handed her any hardships other than the ones she imagined in her own mind. For my father, for me, and for my son, life continued to barrage us with hardships.

Since God was all I felt my son and I had in our lives, I clung to Him and prayed fervently. I needed to believe that God was powerful and that He did hear my prayers and He did love me and my son enough to answer them.

So, for thirty three years of my son's life, I prayed and I prayed for my child. I told God I was fine with anything else that happened to me in this fruitless existence I called life, but please God, just watch over my child.

Now I question, did an ineffective mother pray to an ineffective God and my child died? Am I not good enough, strong enough, wise enough, pious enough for God to have heard my prayers and saved my son?

Or did God open doors I could have walked through to have a better life and did I let my fear of everything hold me back? While my child was alive I felt as though I was holding a delicate piece of glass and was so afraid I would drop the glass and it would shatter. Through all the pain of his young life, I felt my son was that delicate piece of glass and I was so afraid the woes of this world that had been cast against him would shatter him.

And shatter him they did.

And the only place I knew to turn was to God, for I felt as helpless as my father must have felt in the face of evil.

But, my father's children lived.

Mine did not.

And well meaning, devout, sanctimonious Christians tell me not to blame God, so then who do I blame? I blame myself, I fault myself, I play the recording of my child's life over and over and am found wanting in so many places.

And when the self-blame becomes too heavy a burden to bear, I blame God. Just as my father never protected us from the abuse of my mother, so I feel God didn't protect us either.

My father was not an unkind man.

He was just a weak man.

I feel God is not an unkind God.

He is just a powerless God who chose to turn away from us.

That is how I feel.

My mother and my brothers are cruel, hateful, selfish, unloving, uncaring, dishonest people and they have been blessed.

My father, my son and I were not unkind people and we have been cursed.

When I now tell others what my brothers have done to us, they say "they'll get theirs." I don't want them to "get theirs" for revenge is not what I sought. I was thrown into an abusive war I didn't want to be in. It was us against them, and they won.

Evil won.

My son is gone.

Evil won.

And everything I've ever believed has been shattered like the delicate glass I was so tightly holding onto.

And now, I am undone...

And without purpose...

And without direction...

And without a plan...

And what I cherished most in my life was my child and my relationship with God...

Now, I have neither...

And I miss them both...

For without them, I am empty...

And alone...

It was a day to go to the rooftop and suntan. I felt as if I couldn't be around people today and so wanted to be alone. I had resigned myself to spend a day of self-pity and welcomed the darkness.

But God or the universe or just plain happenstance had other plans.

As I lay sun tanning, the wife of the new renters happened by and began speaking to me. Now, I'm nervous around people and find it's like I'm standing on the sidelines watching a performance. Who was it that said, "The whole world is a stage and I'm the principal player." That is sometimes how my new life feels to me.

If I can't avoid small talk, I find I become quite animated and speak quickly, almost as if I have a certain quota of words to fill, and then I can say my goodbyes. If I can just get to the magic number of chitchat and prattle, then I've remained a polite Canadian and can leave.

The head and the heart war within me constantly. My head understands I still need to co-exist with others in this unnecessary world, while my heart questions why. My head understands; my heart doesn't care.

Immediately upon concluding that conversation, my friend, Heidi, appears before me. She is a welcome sight and I never fully understand how lonely I am until I see her or her husband, Peter. They are kind people and while we share the loss of our sons, we also share a caring friendship.

The fact they live the winter in La Penita and I just happened to find this apartment to rent in La Penita was sheer coincidence. Or was it? Did our sons bring us together? Can they even do that, or do we mortals left behind in this vacuous state of semi alive, semi dead need to somehow make sense out of the unimaginable pain we exist in?

So many unanswered questions that will never be answered this side of death.

Heidi stayed for awhile and used my computer to do her business. It was comforting to have someone here with me, and when she left, Kelly the dog and I also left to walk to the village square. Just having Heidi visit made my step a little lighter and my heart a little calmer. It was a small sense of belonging in a world to which I no longer belong.

I am drifting somewhere between this world and the next, with my heart already gone. It is only this earthly body that holds me back, for I want to be with my son.

Kelly and I drifted towards the crying ocean where we always seem to go. This time I determined not to cry. I tried, but didn't succeed, and as Kelly and I sat by the rock bluffs, I cried out to my son and asked him to forgive me. I asked his forgiveness for being so afraid to talk about sad things that I never did. I asked his forgiveness for being so afraid to do anything that I did nothing. I asked his forgiveness for failing him as a mother and not helping when I had the opportunity to do so.

I don't feel forgiven.

I don't feel anything but deep sorrow.

I know it's not my son who has to forgive me for he already has.

I know it's me who has to forgive myself, but how can I when I'm to blame?

I don't deserve to be forgiven and so I carry the burden of my sin.

My son would have long ago taken the burden away.

But then he was a much better person than I could ever hope to be...

Day 10

Did I know? Did some part of me know? I remember Christmas before last. Even though we hadn't spent it together, I went to visit a few months later and took him his presents. He seemed dissatisfied not with the gifts, but with the idea that I had bought him a new razor and some new clothes. Stuffing them in a bag, all the while thanking me, he took his newly acquired possessions to his basement and left them there.

A quick flash jumped to the forefront of my mind and I thought, "He doesn't want new things because he is preparing to take his life, and they will all be wasted then." It was such a horrendous thought that I wouldn't and couldn't entertain it, so quickly pushed it away. After that I was nervous in my speech and watchful in my words and was afraid, so afraid, for he seemed sad; resigned and sad. And what I thought was acquiescence for whatever question I'd ask him, or whatever topic I'd bring up, now that I have the same feeling, was merely a struggle to care.

For now that I'm steeped in a grieving state of mind, all else pales in significance and nothing brings me joy. Sometimes, for others, I will pretend, but deep inside, where my feelings matter, my state of mind is never free from the overpowering grief I bear.

My son carried a great burden of a life filled with hardship and I was helpless to turn back the hands of time and give him the life he should have had. I carry this pain, knowing that to do what he did, he must have been in even greater pain, and I can't endure the thought that who I loved more than life itself couldn't find a way out of his despair.

It rips me in two and I can't seem to get enough air in my lungs to exhale.

This didn't need to be.

And now that it has happened, how can I carry the weight of it? How can I go on?

I sometimes forget he's gone and life seems normal again. It seems acceptable to smile.

But then I remember, and nothing will ever be acceptable again.

Today was market day at the village square. I slept fitfully and unwell and woke up feeling lethargic and unmotivated to do the weekly shopping.

Since my perro needs to pee, I have no choice but to get dressed and go outside. Once there, it is a pleasant saunter to the market. Where only a short week ago, I noticed the poverty and garbage strewn streets, now I sidestep the garbage and see the joy in the laughing children as they play.

Today I felt little joy and my heart was heavy. The sunshine did nothing to alleviate my mood, and what finally got me smiling was seeing the wide berth shoppers gave to Kelly, my dog. She made an imposing figure in the midst of the malnourished dogs you see in Mexico, and many times passersby would stop me and say "grande perro" which means large dog. I would say, "si, mucho grande perro." (very large dog). If only they knew she had the heart of a pussycat and was a gentle giant.

Still, I feel safe and secure walking with her by my side and whatever I thought to fear only a week ago, is no longer any concern. We walk where we please. What else can this world do to me now?

As I wandered the open shops searching for my fruits and vegetables, I spotted t-shirts for sale and one said “Conserve Water. Drink beer.” It made me smile and I started walking towards it, thinking my son, Steve, would enjoy the shirt.

Stopping as quickly as I’d started, it hit me there was no reason to buy him anything anymore. The only thing left to buy my son was a headstone and then I would never need to buy him anything again. Whatever wealth or prosperity or goodness that might come my way will now be wasted, for anything of value was only for him. I can exist with little and now my needs are even less than they were.

What was the use? What was the use of anything?

It was a sad day.

And there was nothing I could do to change what happened.

Not death, God...

Not death...

Anything but that...

Day 11

I feel shaky. I feel as if I am, singlehandedly, holding in a colossal dam that may soon burst. I feel that once it bursts, I won't feel better, but worse. So I hold it in, not knowing the force behind it that may implode me into a thousand pieces.

Right now I don't feel suicidal. While I pray for God to be merciful and take me to be with my son, I know I won't hurry along the process unless a mere will to die can do it. But, if I let this flood of emotions surface, boil and spill over my seemingly calm demeanor, will I go running for the closest bottle of pills? Will I pour them, glutinously, down my throat and catapult myself into oblivion?

I don't know.

So, I hold the dam back. And do what I always do.

I wait.

I wait for something to happen to me, for me, with me, in spite of me. I sit and wait and do not make my own destiny, I do not make my own choices, I do not make my own decisions unless you count a decision to do nothing.

I pray and I hope and I wait.

And waiting has got me where I am today.

For no one made any magical decisions, no one decided to suddenly love us, no one rescued me or helped me or taught me or showed me what direction to go. They all have lives of their own to live, and while we touch each other's lives, and we care about each other, we can't be in each other's back pockets guiding or directing.

And when it came to my son, I also sat and waited. I just waited for him to turn out good and kind and decent and honest and loving, and for all intents and purposes, I succeeded in my wait. He did turn out to be all those things and more. He struggled and worked and tried so hard to be what this world would call a success. He succeeded, too. His friends tell me they looked up to him and commended his soft heart, gentle nature and dry, witty sense of humor.

But, at what cost to self?

Obviously, it came at a price too high to pay, for he paid with his life. Now, anything I may write or think about why he took his own life is only a mother's conjecture and in the end, I don't know what his last thoughts were.

All I do know for sure is he was tired, because he told me. He was tired of struggle, tired of working so hard, tired of being tired. And is that what took my baby away? One day, did he just feel too tired to continue in this world? And where was I? I was in Arizona, probably having the best time I ever had in my life.

And did he listen to me expound the virtues of living in Arizona for the winter, and did he listen to my once harried voice now take on a softness he'd probably never heard before, and did he decide his mom was going to be ok, so it was fine for him to go? For you see, as long as he would have thought I would fall apart, he wouldn't have done this. He needed to know I would survive, and that is why, even in death, he made sure I had a loving dog to look after me.

What he didn't know is, without him, I won't survive.

Once again, this is all an expression of an opinion without sufficient evidence of proof, for the only one who can answer these questions is no longer here to ask.

Last night I dreamt about my son and it was a very vivid dream. There was nothing earthshattering about my dream; we were just visiting together and having innocuous conversations. But I could see his face so clearly and longed to touch my son's face and hug him to me. The dream seemed long and could have been a scene in anyone's house in anyone's life, and I so wanted it to go on and on. A barking dog outside shattered this peaceful sleep and I was thrown into this harsh, cruel world where I continue to exist without my son.

Instantly the aching to be with my child overpowered and the emotions felt too strong to resist. I felt as though I'd been thrown into a vat of slithering reptiles, who would leave my body untouched, but would eat away at my heart and my very soul. I struggled laboriously to escape, but all to no avail, for they were free to claw and chew and devour the very essence of who I was as a human being; of who I was as a mother.

For I tried the best way I knew how.

And I failed...

Today was a day best described as disgruntled. Being rudely awoken from a dream I very much wanted to cling onto left me feeling at loose ends and disturbed.

To the far right of the fishermen's beach Kelly and I walk on were some rock bluffs and I'd been told that just beyond the bluffs was a deserted stretch of beach where you could walk for seven miles. I'd determined today that Kelly and I would climb the bluffs and walk the wide stretch of beach beyond.

As Kelly and I stepped onto the beach now familiar to us, I removed my sandals and let the warm sand massage my toes. Being so used to talking to God before He allowed my world to be destroyed, I asked that He please not let me come across any more snakes. Then, remembering that God and I are no longer friends, I said, "Oh yeah, please no snakes and please protect my child. Oops, no can do, can you, God?"

Instantly I felt a needle prick on the instep of my foot and cried out in pain. Afraid it may have been a needle, for this was not the cleanest beach I'd seen, I looked down to see a dried up prong of the outside of a pineapple sticking out of my foot.

It was as if a loving parent had disciplined a petulant child, and just as a petulant child feels justified in their sense of wrong done to them, so I felt justified in my snarkiness towards God. I understood and while my foot throbbed, I knew my attitude towards God needed some adjustment.

We continued on our way.

As we started to climb, I noticed the pathway up the rock bluffs become steeper and steeper. Rounding a corner I saw not a descent, but an ascent further up the rocks that, if I were to fall, I would fall headlong into the surf below and be dashed against the rocks. Even Kelly looked hesitant and knowing this was not a safe way to go, we returned back to the apartment.

I couldn't find a place of rest for myself today. As I lay sun-tanning on the roof, I wondered how many more days I could waste the hours tanning before my skin turned to leather. I didn't really want a darker tan; I just don't know what to do.

I still don't know what to do.

I'm unhappy here, I'm unhappy there.

I just want a do-over with my son...

Day 12

Maybe I deserve this. Maybe I deserve this painful life I've had to endure. I've pretty well always believed in God and the bible and the scripture where it says "It's given man once to die, and then the judgment", which would show you I'm not a fan of reincarnation or any of those other philosophies.

Now that I've been thrown into this new world that appears somewhat surreal and quite honestly, a massive waste of time, for what good can come of it now that my child is gone, I question everything. I definitely question my religion of choice, for lack of a better word. And yet there is some yearning, deep inside, that still wants to believe in a loving God and justice and fairness and kindness and hope and love. All these emotions that, at this point, are foreign to me, for when grief of this proportion enters your soul, there is little room for anything else.

I'm reading a book by one of my favourite authors and the title is "Saving Fish from Drowning." Anonymously written was a short paragraph explaining how the title came to be. It read: *A pious man explained to his followers: "It is evil to take lives and noble to save them. Each day I pledge to save a hundred lives. I drop my net in the lake and scoop out a hundred fishes. I place the fishes on the bank, where they flop and twirl. "Don't be scared," I tell those fishes. "I am saving you from drowning." Soon enough, the fishes grow calm and lie still. Yet, sad to say, I am always too late. The fishes expire. And because it is evil to waste anything, I take those dead fishes to market and I sell them for a good price. With the money I receive, I buy more nets so I can save more fishes."*

As supposedly logical thinking, intelligent humans, we can rationalize anything, can't we? It is only when something like your child dying happens, that nothing any longer makes sense, and you realize that all your rationalizations were for naught. For what does it matter anymore? What does anything matter when your child is gone? What does any justification, explanation, exoneration, vindication matter anymore?

For you see, I'm keeping a secret. A secret that proves I am guilty of his death. It is a terrible secret and weighs me down. There is no escaping now knowing this secret and while the person who told me is a good friend, I wonder why I needed to know. People should be cautious when dealing with someone in grief. We are so immersed in our pain and raw and fragile and vulnerable that anything that is said can throw us into more darkness than even we thought possible. If you don't know what to say, better to say nothing. This is not about you and your importance in our lives; this is not about you and your being able to "fix it" or "fix us", for there is no fix to something like this. What we need more than to hear your words of wisdom is to talk. We need to talk and talk, and if you keep interrupting us, in trying to help, we forget where we were and need to say the same sentences again. We don't know what we're saying or doing or thinking from second to second, so we've probably already just told you what we are telling you again.

We no longer have the capacity to rationalize or understand that two plus two equals four, for in our new found world we've been catapulted into, two plus two no longer equals four. We've buried our child; we've watched them be put into the ground; we've suffered the worst pain known to mankind. What do you possibly think you could say to make us feel better?

If God can no longer touch our hearts and heal our pain, how, mere mortal man, do you think you can? So, if you truly care for me, just let me talk and let me cry, and hug me when I do. This new grief leaves me unable to distinguish right from wrong, caring from gossip, your sense of duty towards our friendship from true love of me, but someday I will understand. Someday I will figure it out again, and when that someday comes, I will be touched beyond explanation by your willingness to be there for me and to care. Only in that "someday" will I be able to properly thank you, for right now, I am immersed in my grief and can see nothing other than this cavernous pit of my despair.

Today Kelly the dog and I determined to walk the seven mile stretch of beach we were unsuccessful in getting to yesterday. Well, truth be told, I was more determined than Kelly; she was just along for the ride. Or should I say walk?

I knew the general direction to be taken and started along Highway 200, the Mexican equivalent to our freeway and the main passageway in and out of town. As there were rooftop dogs on the other side of the highway, Kelly and I had to walk on the side that had traffic behind us, instead of facing us. While many cars whizzed by me, I made sure Kelly was on the inside and she was more than happy to oblige.

Crossing the busy roadway, we arrived at a trailer park and were able to circumvent it by taking a small side pathway. This pathway had dense jungle to either side and when we reached the clearing that opened to the ocean, I was relieved. To the left of us were the rock bluffs we had tried to climb yesterday and upon seeing them from the opposite direction, I was glad we had turned back.

Nothing was before us but the wide expanse of ocean. I stopped every few hundred yards to take in what I knew to be beauty, but there was no beauty in my soul. What, only a short six months ago, would have made me giddy with glee, now felt like a slap in the face. How can this magnificence exist in a world that no longer held my son? How can the world not stop spinning now that he is gone? How can this be, God? How can this be?

I threw a stick for Kelly and she leapt in the ocean waves, oblivious to anything but the retrieval of her prize, the stick. These waves were not for the fainthearted perro and many times she was swallowed up, only to be propelled towards shore, trusty stick in tow.

I tired of this game long before she did and we continued on our way. After miles of trudging through hot sand and salty water, I felt I'd succeeded in my quest and was content to turn around and began our homeward journey.

Stopping to stare at the ocean and the rushing waves, I wanted some emotion of elation to fill me and willed it to surface, but it was no longer there. I continued watching the receding waves, all the while conscious of my faithful dog beside me.

At one point I unhooked my water bottle from its holder and was trying to loosen the shoulder strap that held it in place. Not noticing anything else, I concentrated on my bottle holder when, without warning or any knowledge it was coming, a colossal wave hit me and covered me to my waist. I struggled to remain on my feet and felt the wet sand give way and the water try to pull me down.

Soaked through to my underclothes, I looked around for Kelly, and there she was, many footsteps above me, and dry as a bone. She was watching. I was not.

Others sense danger. I do not.

Which brings me to my secret.

And once I tell you, then others will know, and you will all see that I am responsible for my son taking his life.

Many tell me all manner of platitudes and deny my feelings of guilt; some say nothing; some ask why I needed to know.

I have no answer.

For you see, while I was wintering in Arizona, I was the happiest I had ever been. Poor health and lung problems had taken me to this winter paradise and I was able to breathe well for the first time in many years.

My dear friends came to visit and, when they saw how happy I was, encouraged me to buy a place there and offered to loan me the money, with no interest. They also were in no hurry to be paid back. It was a dream I couldn't have ever imagined for I lived very frugally and had little resources. Being Canadian, I could only live there six months of the year, but that would be enough. It truly was a dream come true.

In my excitement, I emailed my son and told him I hoped he was doing fine financially because I was going to buy there and if he was ever stuck, I wouldn't be able to help him in any way.

I knew he wasn't doing well financially. He had told me so many times. He had told me how tired he was working three jobs and barely able to cover his mortgage. He had told me and told me, and I didn't listen.

I told him he was a smart boy and would figure it out. God forgive me for I can't forgive myself.

My son knew help was not going to come from me and he had nowhere else to turn to. He had no father, no brother, no sister, no one but me.

Being the unselfish person he was, he emailed me back and said "If it's a good deal, go for it", and he wished me well. Later he called and said to make sure and get it tested for termites as, in that climate, termites were a problem. He knew things I hadn't even thought of, and like always, cared about me more than I seemed to care about him. God forgive me for I can't forgive myself.

After sending me the email wishing me well, he went and purchased a gun. Within a few short weeks, he was gone.

My friends found the receipt with the date imprinted while they were going through his possessions. I wish I didn't know.

Guilty, your honor...

Then, guilty you are...

Day 13

Today I'm going somewhere north with my friends, Pete and Heidi. I woke up tired after tossing and turning most of the night, and don't know that I can put on a happy face. Having lost a son of their own, they understand and are very gentle with me, but I also understand no one else wants to live my grief for long.

My head and my heart continually war with each other and my head understands I have no entitlement to be sad all the time, so many times I pretend and put on a smile. My heart, however, wakes up screaming inside and doesn't want to go through the perfunctory steps of a normal day.

In my old life I persistently put on a happy face and people would draw to me. I hated how lonely I was as a child and that no matter how hard I worked at it, I never felt loved. There were constant criticisms of every move I made, and with what remains of my family today, nothing has changed.

So, I set out to be perfect. An impossible task, but one I undertook. For, in my mind, if I could just be perfect, then maybe I would be loved.

And in my quest for love, I attracted those that wanted me to be perfect also. They couldn't take any negatives to my personality, and when I couldn't keep up the pace of always smiling, always joking, never being in a bad mood or having a bad day; when I would just be a normal person with normal feelings, they would leave.

So then my quest for perfection would be upped a notch and I would try all the harder. I found life so tiring. But, it was my choice. Strive for perfection or be alone?

Sadly, I did the same to my son. But, it wasn't his choice; it was cast upon him by me. I feel nauseous inside thinking of how hard I pushed him to be a perfect little boy; never to throw a tantrum, never to have a bad day. I just wanted him to be loved.

For you see, before he was born, my husband said he felt no love for me or our unborn child, so he left. Then, when my son was three days old, my older brother said my baby was demon possessed and needed an exorcism.

While still in hospital, my son developed jaundice, as many babies do, but when they put him under the ultra violet light, the bandage over his eyes was not affixed so his eyes were burnt. They pussed over and formed scabs and my baby's eyes didn't open for three months. My mother told me God was punishing me for not doing everything she said, and so God had made my baby blind. I was a young girl, just turned twenty-three, and knew nothing of God and his ways, so would imploringly beseech God to protect my baby and make me blind instead.

My baby wasn't blind but had problems with vision for the rest of his life.

When he was ten days old, on his first Christmas on earth, my brother, my mother and others came to the home I had shared with my ex-husband and performed an exorcism on my baby.

They were evil.

I was alone, and just wanted to be loved.

My older brother never did show love to my son and was always cruel to him. When my son died, I emailed my brother and told him the time to be kind to my son was while he was still alive, and to please respect my wishes and not come to the funeral. Steve, my son, would have been proud of me, for it was the first time I ever spoke up to my brother.

It should have been many more times that I spoke up to him.

I just wanted to be loved.

And the only one who did is gone...

If my son were still alive, today would have been a perfect day. Heidi and Pete, along with their friend, Paul, picked me up in the morning and off we went to the beautiful seaside resort of Chacala. The restaurants were all set up ocean-side and many peddlers were selling their wares. It was definitely conducive to the tourist trade and you couldn't help but get caught up in the jovial, holiday mood.

We sat, watching the waves of the small inlet and ate our lunch with the ocean breeze gently blowing; not too hot and not too cold. Pete is a great jokester and had been telling me jokes since we'd met. I used to love telling jokes, but now, when I try, the words get stuck in my throat. How can I make someone else laugh when my son had so little to laugh about? How can I laugh when my son is gone? To me it is disrespectful and dishonorable and when I do hear the sound of my laughter, I instantly feel chagrined by my lack of respect, and wonder what sort of creature I have become that I can laugh only short months after burying my son. How could I? And yet sometimes I do.

Today was one of those days. I so desperately needed a break from the grief.

Haltingly and cautiously I began to tell Pete a joke. The words trembled as they passed through my lips and I doubted they would get to the punch line at the end. Halfway through I wanted to stop, but something inside caused me to persevere. When the joke ended and Pete and Heidi laughed, I felt a moment, or was it just a spark, of life within me.

As he continued to tell me jokes and I began to tell more, I relished and welcomed the feeling of life that began to grow within me. Today, just today, I needed a break from the grief.

And I took one.

After lunch, we swam in the ocean and then proceeded, through jutted road, onto a mountain top hot springs. Basking in the warm mineral water, I felt a calm soothe my tired soul. Heidi swam over to me and began to speak of our boys, and how they needed to find a place without pain, and so they did. The tears sprang to my eyes and I wanted to run away. I knew I would break down crying if this conversation were to continue, so asked her to stop.

I just needed a break from the pain.

Did my son feel the same way only to a much higher degree?

My heart aches for him, for he never got a break from the pain.

Day 14

You never escape the grief; you only think you do. I don't believe anyone was ever meant to feel this degree of pain, so everything in you fights to run away. But, where do you run to? Where do you find a place of solitude that gives you a brief respite from the grief? Nowhere. You only think you do.

Returning to the empty apartment after a day with my friends brought the emptiness which has now become my life into focus. I realized this is the reality of my life and I need to make peace with the fact I may always be alone. For most of my life I have fought the concept and would not even entertain the possibility that someday I wouldn't be surrounded by friends and loved ones and would achieve the just recompense for years of hardship and strife.

I was surrounded by friends and loved ones, all right.

At my child's funeral...

What a fool I was to believe that anything good could come our way.

What a colossal fool I was...

The perplexing part is that the saddest day of my life came on the heels of what was probably the happiest time I'd ever experienced and I often think of a conversation I had while hiking in Arizona with my friend, Brad.

After miles and miles of hiking together you pretty well run through every subject of conversation and eventually religious beliefs enter in. He believed in meditating, gurus, and had even visited an ashram at one time. While I knew nothing of his faith, he knew nothing of mine, but we were both open to hearing what the other had to say.

I told him I believed in God, Jesus and the bible and practiced living my faith in my daily life. Not wanting to tell my new friend the extent of the horror my child and I had lived through, I started with the most recent events of my life, and told him I'd had a pretty rough last few years. Poor health kept me housebound to a certain degree and as the problems were due to my lungs, taking a deep breath was difficult to do.

I told my new friend there is a scripture in the bible that says, "God will not give you more than you are able," and one day, after being sick with pneumonia for the entire winter, I stood in my kitchen, looked up to the heavens, quoted the scripture to God, and told him I thought He may have overshot here, for this was more than I was able to endure. Little did I know what was in store for me beyond the horizon.

Within a very short period of time, I felt as though I was swept up and things began to unfold beyond my control. It seemed doors started to open and my only choice was to walk through them or not. I walked through those open doors and started a pathway that went from a mere existence to a full and rich life, if only for a short time.

The opportunity to winter in Arizona came upon me and everything just fell into place. I was used to working very hard to achieve anything and finding a roommate to travel with me, a wonderful place beyond my expectations to live in in Arizona, friends from Canada who would also be wintering in a city close by, seemed too good to be true. And probably was.

It was all unfolding, with little effort from me, and I was excited about the future for the first time in a very long time.

I continued telling my friend that when I arrived in Arizona, I still had difficulty breathing and talking at the same time, and would gasp when I tried to say a word. Within a week, I awoke feeling happy and wondered why.

Then I realized I could breathe easier, my chest didn't hurt as much, and the aches and pains that lived in me in Canada were gone. How could I not feel joy in my heart?

I've always believed and said many times, that peace, joy and contentment have to come from within. I remember my dad saying, "You can't run away from yourself, for wherever you go, you'll be there." I believed and understood that concept and knew my sadness in life always came from outward circumstances, but I'd determined, while still very young, to not let the "sad" permeate my soul. I determined, while still very young, to find a way to overcome my circumstances and prove to the world and to myself that life would never pull me down to where I couldn't get up again.

What a fool I was.

While my friend didn't know all the circumstances of our life, I encompassed a lifetime into a few words that my son and I had lived through hell. We both struggled and persevered and fought hard to not let our circumstances drag us down and then I told my friend the biggest lie I'd ever spoken. I told him we had made it; my son and I. We had made it and life was now on an upswing. We had survived unheard of abuse and we had come out the other side, for surely the joy I felt here in Arizona had shown me we'd endured much tribulation and came through the other side to a life that now can only be filled with happiness.

I didn't know, at that time, that what I was speaking was a lie, and truly believed my son and I had overcome. I truly believed God had somehow intervened on our behalf and all my prayers were answered. I truly believed that thirty-three years of praying for my child had paid off and I would return to Canada where the two of us, while living individually, would have a fresh start. This was just the beginning of our new life.

How right I was.

It was a new life; one I could never have imagined.

What a fool I was...

Was God looking down on me thinking I was a fool, too?

My head knows He wasn't, but my heart has a difficult time trying to understand.

Today was a sad day for me. I woke up too early and felt lethargic and unmotivated the entire day. Thankfully there was nothing planned and no one to see, so I could wander aimlessly through the day thinking about my son.

Where is he now?

Can he see me?

Does he understand how sad I am?

Does it make him sadder?

Can we reach each other?

Is there any way he can communicate with me?

Has he already and I just can't hear?

Do the things that happen to me where I feel protected and as if someone else is watching over me have anything to do with him?

When I'm sad and Kelly the dog comes and nudges my hand so I pet her, is Kelly somehow being guided by my son?

Am I just imagining and hoping and making things up because I so badly can't bear the thought of no contact with him ever again?

Do I wish upon a star?

Do I pray to a God who might not exist?

Do I hope someday a peace will fill my soul?

Do I wait to die?

What do I do when my child is no longer here?

Day 15

Two weeks I've been here; two weeks since the plane touched down on Mexican soil and Kelly and I disembarked. Two weeks can seem a lifetime, and yet two weeks can seem but a moment.

In this short or long while, depending on how you look at it, I've learnt a lot. I've learnt I don't like to be alone and when sadness surrounds, I wish there was someone to comfort. My friends say that maybe I'm trying too hard to feel the pain in hopes of diving in, both feet first, and then hopefully coming through the other side with some semblance of sanity and a desire to live. My one friend, when I told of how lonely I was, said, "Let's see. You wanted to go somewhere isolated where there were no tourists, where you can walk the beach alone, where you can cry as much as you want, and now that you have exactly what you wanted, you're feeling lonely and alone?"

Yes, that would pretty well sum it up.

Right now I feel as though I'm running a race with the pain; I want to be one footstep ahead and not cry anymore. I want to just be a normal person with normal day to day happenings and I don't want to be the mother who has just lost her only child.

I don't want to be her.

But I am...

And somehow I want to run away, escape, put my hands over my ears so I can't hear the sound of my heart breaking, put my hands over my eyes so I can't see my world falling apart, put my hands over my mouth so the moaning sobs no longer tear out of me.

I don't want to be a mother whose child could find no more comfort, no more caring, no more hope in this comfortless, uncaring, hopeless world and so chose to leave.

But I am...

I don't even want to write anymore. What purpose can it achieve? I don't feel better writing about my grief anymore. At first it did bring some small comfort to pour out my heart and I thought it gave me a purpose for being, but now I don't want to sit in front of my computer and talk about my day. Who cares? Who really cares about my day? I don't care about my day. Why should you care? What possibly could be hoped to gain from knowing the anguish of one person's broken heart?

Today I went to the town of Bucerias with my friends, Heidi and Pete. Thank God for them because some days I can't bear the weight of my own company and that seems to be when they show up. We went to visit other friends of theirs in Bucerias, which is about twenty minutes from the city of Puerta Vallarta.

While Heidi and Pete did the business they had to do, I spent part of the day with their friend, Monica. She and her husband are from Germany and winter in Mexico. They have a beautiful home they own and appear to live very well. All of a sudden it bothered me that I live so frugally and exist with so little. It bothered me that I rarely complained about my lack in life. It bothered me that, if I only have one life to live, it sure wasn't much of a life. It bothered me that what others wouldn't put up, I take as my due and have so often done without. It bothered me that people take for granted their children will visit, give them grandchildren, outlive them, and that I can no longer have that.

All of a sudden, every lack in my life bothered me and I realized there were so many things I did without.

And it bothered me that while my child was still alive, none of these things bothered me for it was only his safety and happiness that were of importance.

And it bothered me that even the little I'd hoped for in life, which was my child to be happy and healthy, I couldn't even have.

And it bothered me that I have to know what this pain feels like, and there is no good reason for it.

It all just bothered me and I observed these kind and wonderful people, all the while thinking I was no less than them, and yet had lived as if I was.

Now, it all mattered and it all bothered me and there was no calm and there was no peace and there was no joy.

And I can tell I'm holding in the tears because I just want to escape further from the grief, but all I see is my child's face and all I can feel is the hopelessness and despair he must have been in, and all I can do is try to exist, while not wanting to.

And I know soon I am going to break down.

But, not today God, just not today.

I want a normal day...

Day 16

The break is over; no more break for Nina. Nowhere left to escape the pain, for the tears now come in my dreams. I can feel myself wanting to hold back from crying and just needing to take a breath without feeling the stab of grief, but it is always there, waiting to embrace me and cover me like a heavy shroud of sorrow.

I see my son's face before me and notice the kindness in his eyes. I see him shrug his shoulders and hear him with his witty sayings that would have me in hysterics, while he didn't even seem to bat an eye. I see him pet the dog one last time as he put her in the kennel, hoping, or knowing she would be found. I see him put the gun to his head and feel his anguish to be able to do such a thing. I see him lying there for four days because it took that long before his neighbors noticed no movement in his house and called the police. I see too much horror for a mother to absorb, so I want to run.

I ran to Mexico, but the pain and the grief followed me here. I ran away to drug induced sleep, but the vision of my son as a baby, as a child, as a young adult, followed me there. I ran away into pushing the thought that he is gone far into the recesses of my mind, but, without warning, I see, hear, or touch something that reminds me of him and reminds me he is gone.

I was told you have to embrace the grief and walk through it in order to heal. Who knows that for sure? Who is this expert that says that is the way to deal with this? There is no way to deal with this. This is such a horrendous experience that there is no reprieve, there is no right way, there is no escape. Then I was told I need to deal with it the best way I can. That makes more sense to me, but still sentences me to a lifetime of grieving for my child. What could possibly motivate me to want to stay on this earth if that is the life sentence now passed down to me? My friend says time will heal and while I will never forget, there will be moments where I'll forget and the pain won't be as bad. I told her those were just words to me and felt angry she would say those words because to me, that meant my son was not worth grieving for very long. She was trying to help but I wanted her to stop talking for I could feel the unshed tears of the past few days well up inside and I didn't want to lose control. I just want everyone to leave me alone. Or do I? For when I am alone, the grief seems intolerable and I wish there was someone just to hold me and let me cry.

Last night I dreamt about my son and was crying in my dreams. I awoke, with a start, about 5 a.m. and was troubled with a sense of unrest. Not knowing what else to do, I brought Kelly the dog in bed with me and cuddled close to her. Even though it wasn't human contact, it was contact with something alive and breathing, and as Kelly cuddled in closer, licked my ear, and started snoring, I was strangely comforted and knew my son would have known I'd need her to get me through. But, to get me through what? This is something I will never get through. This is something I will never get over. And if time does eventually heal, then I will write another journal and let you know. I will then feel duly chastised for my obstinate resistance to advice and tell the well-wishers they were right.

Until that time, I resolutely believe nothing will change because I won't let it change. I don't want to get better from this. I don't want to improve. I don't want to find a purpose for living.

My son didn't get to. Why should I?

I didn't do much of anything today. Slept fitfully and restlessly, so then was unmotivated to do much of anything else. I know I'm holding in the tears, and when I hold in the emotion, then find I'm also too lethargic to do anything else. It takes a lot of energy to hold back the torrent of tears that are waiting to be unleashed.

The only time I left the complex was to take Kelly for her pee. She stays by my side and watches me wherever I go. If this is her job, then she is doing it well.

Suntanned on the rooftop and watched a lot of television. Made dinner and am trying to watch what I eat so I can maybe lose a few pounds. But, after dinner, even though I wasn't hungry, I opened a bag of potato chips in hopes they would make me feel better. The old me used food like a drug and the new me was trying to get the same high from my potato chip addiction. It didn't work. Nothing worked. I felt no release from the pain.

Just as I could feel myself sink into self-pity I knew I would have a difficult time crawling out of, my neighbor, Sharon, knocked on my door and invited me to the rooftop to visit with her and her husband, Alex. I had told Sharon yesterday what happened to my son, although not all the details, and she told me I could talk to them whenever I needed. I'd asked them if we could go to dinner in the next town over, Rincon de Guayabitos, and plans have been made for the three of us to do so tomorrow.

I found conversation difficult and struggled to keep up with their stories. I didn't want to hear about their cat being run over and unintentionally say, "that's nice," or hear about their son getting married and accidentally say, "oh, that's a shame." I try to keep some pretense of understanding and for the most part, think I fake my interest quite well. It's not that I don't think other people's lives aren't interesting; it's that I no longer care about much.

After a respectable amount of time, I excused myself politely and came back to my room where I could wallow in private.

This life, this life, this life...

It is not one I would wish on anyone...

Day 17

I had mentioned in a previous chapter there was a mirror directly behind my laptop computer where I sit and write about my day. At that time I thought the woman looking back at me may have been pretty at one time in her life. Now, I look up quickly from my composition and see a haggard face with eyes that appear to be bottomless in their misery and anguish.

I understand now why some cultures cover the mirrors if there has been a close death in the family, for I cannot bear to look into my eyes. For my eyes are the eyes of my child. While his muscular build and tall frame was due to my ex-husband, his facial features came courtesy of me. And when I would look into his eyes, I would see my own, as now when I look into my eyes, I see his.

The yearning for my son, at those moments, is beyond explanation or comprehension. The torment and torture of my soul seems to be without end.

Maybe I do deserve this. Maybe I made so many choices to sit back and do nothing in my life, that I deserve to be living this. Maybe, when there were opportunities to help my son, and I was either too timid or too afraid or too nervous or too stupid or too unsure of what to do, so did nothing, maybe I helped bring about this ultimate consequence.

An excellent example presented itself the other day. My friend from Canada doesn't have internet at her house, so came to use mine. As they have helped me in so many ways, I told her she was welcome to use it any time. However, when we would meet, she would have just come from the internet cafe, or from other friends who also had internet. When we went to Bucerias together, I casually mentioned that she could still use my internet to communicate with family and friends back home. She responded by saying that was very nice, but she found my internet too slow, so would be using other means.

I told her since another couple moved into the apartment complex and shuffled around the router which hooks up the internet, it has really slowed down and sometimes just shuts off completely. As this is my evening entertainment and only way of communication with the world at home, I would then not be able to do so.

My friend said I should complain to the landlord for if I don't, then I will never get helped or have it change. That concept had not even occurred to me for I thought it too small a problem to concern my landlord about. I thought my inconvenience was a small trifle of trivial importance and so would just put up and do the best I can.

I came to realize that is how I have spent most of my life, and, God forgive me, how I taught my son to view the world.

Further introspection made me realize, however, that when you are dealing with your house burning down, you are not concerned with whether your nail polish is peeling and should be redone. I am speaking figuratively and not literally, but the main objective of this story is to say that, in my life, my proverbial house was always burning down.

It would take a lifetime to tell a lifetime, so I am briefly touching on years of abuse. As this book is about my son, my grief and our life together, I don't want to give a lot of airtime to a hatefully abusive family that gave him not a moment's peace. Yet I do realize it could leave the reader wondering what I am alluding to. Hence the conundrum, but for now, it has to suffice that because of the terrible abuse brought about by my family, my son and I ran for our lives and at one time, were actually in hiding in Ontario, which is 3000 miles from where our home was in British Columbia. We lived in a tent, I ran out of food, and my poor little boy became a man before he ever got a chance to be a child.

He learnt very early on in life that inconveniences like slow internet paled in significance with not having enough food to eat that day. He learnt very early in life that a day not being abused by my family meant he was having a good day.

Line upon line, precept upon precept. I so worried that all the years of being cast aside, told to run, told to be quiet and tell no one anything for you never knew what danger lurked, shaped and formed him into the man who could not find a way out other than to leave this world.

Do you now understand why I am responsible? I was his mother and should have protected him more and watched out for him more and taught him he counted more, but I was so busy trying to put out the burning house I had no time for a little boy.

I met his outward needs and kept him physically safe, but at what cost emotionally? And if my child were alive today and flourishing, of course, this story would not be being written. Another story would be written by me, one where I would be recounting a terrible life of abuse only to reassure the reader we had overcome. We had beaten the odds and my child and I were well and thriving in a world of beauty. That is the story I had hoped to write. That is now the story I will never be able to tell.

In writing this journal I had hoped to write about the people, the culture, the things that inspired me to go on while in Mexico, but after only a few short weeks, I appear to have lost interest in everything and exist lonely and alone. As I walk the beach with my perro, I take notice of what I consider newsworthy goings on and make a mental note to write about them later in the day. By the time I reach my apartment and sit down to write, I've forgotten what I'd seen, for everything is of little relevance to me and nothing brings me joy.

After the first sunset at the beach, I've gone to see a few more, but none have compared. Or is it just my mood that no longer sees beauty anywhere? I have no desire to take any pictures nor do I want any taken of me.

Yesterday I had made plans with my new neighbours in the complex to go to the nearby city of Rincon de Guayabitos. They asked me what I wanted to do and I said I need somewhere with noise as I've been spending most evenings alone in my room. Today, the wife, Sharon, came over to tell me they couldn't go as her husband, Alex, was sick with a cold. When you only know a few people and are mostly alone, it is very disappointing to have someone cancel on you, for then I knew it would be another evening spent alone with Kelly the dog.

Since I haven't left the complex for almost two days, I decided to take Kelly to see the sunset before dinner. Every time I'm at the oceanfront this time of day, I see an elderly couple sitting on their lawn chairs, waiting for the sun to go down. She always brings either needlepoint or mending and he patiently sits beside her, seemingly enjoying the quiet of the day. There is a comfortableness that emanates from them and sometimes I watch them as much as I watch the sunset. It would be so nice to have someone to share life with, and yet I know I'm too broken to even consider such a thing.

I sat there today, watching the sun go down, realizing I was one step closer to the day I would die, and while that thought causes me no distress, the fact that I may be all alone when it happens leads me to wonder how this became my life?

I have all the questions.

But the answers somehow have passed me by....

Day 18

I'm bored and lonely; and lonely and bored. Feeling trapped inside myself, I can't seem to venture out very far and so have sentenced myself to spend most of my time here alone.

Since I've spent most of my life alone, and thought that was intolerable, this is a feeling without words.

I've also discovered if you don't cry during the day, the tears will come at night, and catch you like a thief while you sleep.

As I've never buried a child before, and had no warning, no trial run, no time to prepare, I'm not altogether sure what I'm to be feeling or doing. When I laugh I feel guilty, but sometimes it's as if my very soul needs the air laughter brings. Since I'm beating myself up for every mistake I'd made as a mother and have already found myself guilty of his death, it's a pretty paltry existence I lead. People say time will heal somewhat, but I will never forget. I desperately want the time to pass so that maybe one small iota of the pain will pass. Right now, though, I can't ever imagine feeling anything but what I feel.

The haggard old lady stares back at me from the mirror over my laptop and I wonder what I could have done different? So many things; so many other choices that may have saved his life. It's like I was on a personal pathway to destruction and I do wonder if life really is fifty percent luck and fifty percent what we choose to do with it.

I've felt afraid all of my life; afraid of my mother, afraid of my brothers, afraid to be alone, afraid to never be loved, afraid people wouldn't like me, afraid to say, do, feel, or act upon the wrong thing. I feel as though most of my life I've sat waiting for the next bomb to drop, all the while struggling so hard to make a better life.

How do we become that way? We're not born afraid. Or are we? It appears I was and somehow I rationalized in my mind that if I could be so good, and so kind, and so honest, and so fair, and never demand and never get angry and never hurt anyone, that life or God would say, "Now, look at her. What a fine human being she is. Let's just make sure nothing too bad comes her way." In hindsight, I see the ridiculousness of my thought process, but I didn't know what else to do. I didn't know how else to protect my child and myself, and so thought I could cheat the odds and by being the best I could be, save us from anything worse.

I was wrong.

But, still don't know how to be right.

I still don't know what to do different.

I'm no longer afraid of much, but I am afraid to be alone.

It would appear this has been my main motivator most of my life; to rid myself of this deep, desolate solitude I've somehow fallen into as a child, and have been unsuccessful in crawling out of, even as an adult.

For thirty-three years I belonged; I belonged with my child and thought he belonged with me. For thirty-three years I had a purpose, a sense of love, a wonderment that such an amazing child could come out of me.

For thirty-three years, while the rest of the world still frightened me, I had a safe port in the storm to cling to, and to know my life meant something, and I had made a difference in this world by producing this wonderful man.

I know I'm not wrong in my description of him.

He deserved so much better than he got...

Day 19

I had met two women from Canada on the beach about a week ago. They were very friendly and with only a two week vacation here in Mexico, they wanted to see and do and experience all there was.

Yesterday, as I was feeling about as low as I could go, they appeared on my doorstep and wondered if I'd be interested in sharing their last night with them and going to a karaoke restaurant for dinner. I about knocked them over in my enthusiasm to be out the door.

Walking to the restaurant I wondered how I would be and if I would even tell them the real reason I was here, seeing as I probably would never see them again. Entering the restaurant, we quickly were surrounded by the lively conversation and laughter, and I wanted to cringe and run away. Politeness and a lifetime of living to not make others uncomfortable kept me rooted to my seat.

Then, I did what I am ashamed to admit in this chapter.

I almost became the old me.

I was animated and lively and wanting to meet people and experience life. Like a drowning swimmer, as she propels herself upwards, her lungs bursting for air, so I felt in this karaoke restaurant. I wanted to break free of the lead encased bodycast I'd donned only short months ago, and wanted to be like everyone else, and more.

I'd experienced the saddest sad, the cruelest cruel, the grief of all griefs, and know I came to Mexico to run away, if only for a moment. As my son's face would swim before me, I would push it away. God forgive me. I am a terrible mother.

I did things I've never done before. In my previous life, content to be an observer of others while they danced and sang, I envied those who were uninhibited and free. This time I became one of them and when the girls suggested singing karaoke, I readily agreed. We were awful and before I would have been mortified and horrified; well, truthfully I wouldn't have even gone up. Now, I say what more can you do to me, world, nothing matters, who cares? I wish I would have been more like that before.

I sense some reading this and saying, "She's healed." I'm here to tell you, she's not.

While back in Canada, I had watched an Oprah show where she interviewed the parents of three young children who were killed in a car collision. The father said something that spoke to my heart. He said that when they would take a moment of normalcy and maybe laugh or tell a joke or go out for dinner, people would say they were healing well. He further said it was an insult to a grieving parent for it puts the parent, along with their grief, in a box they can't get out of. He said there is no way to understand what losing a child feels like unless it has happened to you, but telling a grieving parent they'll be fine is like a slap in the face. The grieving parent needs to figure out if and when they will be fine, or if they won't be.

No one understands how hard we are trying to make you comfortable and to not be screaming our pain and shedding our tears and bemoaning our lives, so to tell us we're fine shows us we were too good an actress. For now that is what I am when I'm with you; an actress. In some ways, that is what I've always been. But now, I don't want to expend the energy to find out who I really am, for I'm a mother who no longer has a child, and I'm a throwaway person without a purpose in this life.

As I was leaving my new friends, one of them said she envied me for being able to stay here longer. I was shocked to hear those words and wondered how a person could forget my plight long enough to actually be in a place of envy? Yes, yes, yes, I'm supposed to be understanding and forgiving and know that everyone is doing the best they can, and people say stupid things, and blah, blah, blah.... Maybe people should be a little more careful what they say to me, too. To tell a grieving mother she is envied is cruel, no matter how you look at it. But I kept silent, hugged them goodbye and walked back to my apartment and my waiting perro.

Throughout the night I was plagued with guilt and woke up many times feeling as if I was the ultimate betrayer. While this guilt I feel helps no one, won't bring my son back, only eats away at me even in my sleep, I can't seem to let go of it. For what's on the other side? Acceptance that my son is gone? I don't know. This is new and unchartered territory for me; I don't know how to be, so I just am.

Today I feel tired.

Tired of it all...

Day 20

It's interesting to see this new me unfold. Today is the first day I didn't get up in the morning and start writing my thoughts, my feelings, and my sorrow. I procrastinated all day and finally, in the evening, sat down to write.

I've been told grief comes and goes in waves and you take a break; then it hits you like a shot-put to the knees, and down, down, down you go. I hate to think I'm a normal grieving mother, as I feel there is nothing normal about this. If others have gone before me and lived this grief, for someone, somewhere had to coin the phrase "normal grieving mother", then that must mean there are more of you to come, and this is a devastation I would wish on no one. No one at all.

How can this be happening?

How can my child be gone?

How, God, how?

I've decided to make friends with God again, although I doubt I will ever feel the innocence and trust I felt for him in my former life. It was too lonely without God to talk to, and I may yet again decide He has no place in my life, but for now, I will take all the resources I can get. I just don't know who God is anymore. The God I thought I knew was kind and loving and let my son live. I believed the scriptures that said God was the husband to the husbandless, the father to the fatherless, and I thought He was keeping us safer than this world was letting us be. It still would appear to me He has no power, even when His children pray.

Today is a day without reprieve. The last two days I so desperately wanted to feel normal again and live a normal life so pushed away the very essence of who I now am as a person. I pushed away the mother's heart who, while she failed her son in so many ways, deeply loved him, nonetheless. I pushed away this person I have become who is conscious, every moment of the day, that her son no longer walks this earth. I pushed away the mother who, in her mind's eye, only sees her son, a gun, and the torment he must have felt to pull the trigger. I pushed away my reality and ran to a fantasy.

I sang karaoke for the first time in my life. While to some it might be meaningless, to me it was a colossal step of freedom from always wondering what others were thinking about me. I laughed with strangers and wanted the night to go on, for when I came back to this apartment I now view as home, my reality met me at the door.

Last night I asked my neighbours, Sharon and Alex, if they would go for dinner and maybe dancing. I wanted the fantasy to continue and no longer wanted my reality to hold me captive.

I could feel the dissolution of my resolve to continue the merry go round ride I was on. Faster, faster, faster, if I could just go faster, I may outrun my grief, but the faster I ran, the more speed the grief attained, until I realized it was permanently attached to me, and I would never escape it. There was nowhere to run. I ran to Mexico, how much farther can I go?

The dinner was fine, the company was fine, but like a boiling cauldron, my unshed tears and unsettled emotions rose within me. My inside screamed, "Not yet, please not yet", while my outward appearance showed nothing amiss. How much longer could I keep this up? I didn't want to start screaming or burst out crying with my new friends in a restaurant full of people. Run faster, Nina, run, run, run.

Maybe the despair won't catch up to you. But it's all around me. How do I escape?

We walked the village square where music played, and went for ice cream, but my heart was heavy. It was time to call it a night and go home where loneliness, grief, and despair waited to welcome me home.

Sharon and Alex invited me for breakfast in the morning as they were going with a group of friends. Longing to join in the normalcy of a Sunday in Mexico, I told them I may, but if I'm not downstairs in the morning, to go without me. I knew I wouldn't be going, for the tears were surfacing and wouldn't be abated much longer.

I held out till morning and awoke feeling tired, restless, and heavy hearted. It seems holding my feelings in drains me of all energy so I feel unmotivated to do much of anything. It also seems that trying to live like the normal people, who still have their children, drains me of energy, too. Since I had been endeavoring to do both these things, I felt as though my body was now confined to the bed and moving became an insurmountable task.

Lazing around in my pajamas until noon, I searched for comfort in emails from my friends. While I am blessed with knowing wonderful people, nothing soothed the ache inside. Finally, as Kelly the dog has to do her business, I got dressed and took her for a walk. The walk lightened my mood so we continued on to the beach, arriving at my crying ocean. Slowly, we turned around and headed back.

Restless and frustrated, donning my bathing suit, I went upstairs to tan. Not able to lie still, the pool became my next undertaking. It seemed as though I was hiding from the monster of misery that would soon come to roost and ruin my day.

As I lay back on the roof, the tears erupted and would not recede. They finally won out and there was nothing but tears and heartbreak for the rest of my day.

So many times I can't find words to express how I'm feeling, and feel frustrated to the point of almost no longer wanting to try. I know there is still so much more inside that is needing to come out, and sense that in holding those emotions back, I am holding back so many more. It's as if I'm in a large plastic bag, securely fastened, and am fighting so hard to break through before the air is taken out of me forever. I've felt like this so many times in my past, but never more than now.

Helpless, hopeless, frustrated, unable to express, unable to properly feel, unable to enunciate, unable to escape the doom that is and always was my life, unable to ever see a future without pain and sorrow...

This is no life.

But only a mere existence.

I asked God today why I have to stay and my son had to go?

And received no answer.

Day 21

Today was another day where I've waited till late evening before I started writing. I still want to continue my chapter a day but it sometimes seems pointless to me. What is there to say? I briefly considered changing the title to "A Grieving Mothers Guide to Beating Herself Up in Mexico", for that is how it appears. I feel as if there is no positive, no encouragement, no hope, no future, no contentment and only guilt, remorse and pain. So, why write?

Because I don't know what else to do.

I'm lonely here. I'm lonely everywhere. When I meet people I feel awkward, needy and shy. I never know what kind of emotional day it will be, so hesitate to make future plans. When I ask someone to do something and they say they are already busy, I feel sensitive, vulnerable and am sure it's me they don't want to be with.

This sure wasn't the girl who lived in Tucson, Arizona last winter. People drew to me and I to them. Life was frivolity, laughter and each day was looked forward to with anticipation. Friends are still writing me from there saying they are doing and seeing things I introduced them to, for, before I left Canada, I'd researched the entire state, along with the route down, and had adventures awaiting us at every turn of the road, and every turn of the calendar day.

Now, I feel lost; so lost and alone. How do I fill a day? Who would want to be with me to fill a day? Kelly the dog loves me and wants to be with me, but I long for human companionship and yet feel I have nothing to give. When I laugh, I grieve doubly the next day. For how can I be laughing when my child lays in the ground? Who would want to be with someone who talks that way? Before my child was gone, I didn't want to be with someone who talked that way. And yet, that is the reality that is my life. Death is no longer something to fear, but rather a welcome friend. I am too tired to want to go on; I am too tired to want to try again.

Last night I lay awake for many hours because the tears would not stop. Today they want to surface again, but I push them away. Restless and unrefreshed from a sleepless night, I awoke to the sun shining, roosters crowing and the clatter and clamor of life being lived. What to do with this day?

I decided to take Kelly the dog and walk the busy freeway to see my friends, Heidi and Pete. Since they had also lost a son a few years back, some days we comforted one another, and some days we brought about more pain. I watched them live a full and rich life and yet, many times saw the beginnings of unshed tears. It wrenched my heart to know the pain of losing my son would never leave me and would always hang over me. I don't want to go on.

They have another child, a grandchild, each other; while I have no one. How did I come to a place where I have no one but a dog my son left me? How did my son come to a place where he felt there was no one he could reach out to, or if he did reach out, how is it no one reached back and were able to comfort him? How did we end up so alone with only each other to love? And now, how do I continue without my heart?

Kelly and I spent the day with Heidi and Pete and I do care deeply for my new friends. But they know many other people besides me and have a busy and active life, and I know I can't be with them all the time. I want to be with someone because this is such a lonely journey and a frightening one as well. It is inconceivable to imagine this is the rest of my life, and yet what in my past has ever shown me it will be different?

Nothing.

So, I am tired today. I feel weary and heartsick and exhaustion has settled over me like a fog. I want to break out of this slump I'm in and maybe tell a joke. I want to hear laughter that is my own. I want to live. And yet my child has only been gone seven months. How can I hope to feel any joy?

If this feeling continues where I'm finding writing more of a chore than a place where I can sort through my thoughts and maybe find some semblance of understanding or a purpose to go on, I may stop writing altogether.

I just don't know why I bother and struggle to make sense of any of this. Before I always believed something good could come out of something bad. Nothing good will ever come of this.

Day 22

I sometimes wonder if I'm a little too hard on myself. While parts of me scream a resounding yes, other parts determine I have not yet even begun to feel the full magnitude of the mind numbing pain.

When this just happened I appeared unable to hold much in and acted on instinct, rather than conscious thought. Having two friends, who I cared deeply about, end our friendship shortly after the funeral, left me confused and uncertain as to what I'd said or done. Paramount in my mind was the thought my child was gone, and all else paled in significance.

I'd spent my entire life endeavouring to be as nice as I could be. I'd even jokingly say that my need to have as little drama as possible in my life had led me to a place where if I liked blue and you liked green, well then I would change my mind and also like green. I'd spent my life as a chameleon, ever changing with the mood of others. My thoughts, hopes, fears were not just secondary, they were non-existent if it inconvenienced anyone else.

The only time I would open up was if I met someone I trusted. Then, like a torrential downpour, my emotions, thoughts and sentiments would all be exposed. There was so much bottled up inside, and I lived my life as though an actor on a stage; always "on", that when there was a kind, listening ear, I enveloped the warmth, caring and closeness of the person involved. Since my life was so tumultous, sometimes the life story I would allow to unravel would be too much for the other person to bear, believe or understand. I never lied. I never needed to. My truth was so much more horrific than any lie I could ever fabricate. So was the life of my son.

I had taught him to hold it all in, just as I held it all in. I didn't want people to view us as those two who led a life of abuse. I wanted people to view us as those two who are funny, witty, kind, gentle, loving, and a success in life. When he would want to talk about the down times, the sadness he felt, the fear of losing his house, the sore ankle, or any other such normalcy of life, I couldn't bear to hear his pain, no matter how miniscule, so would turn a deaf ear and a blind eye. Then, doing what we've always done, he would start to joke around and talk about nonsensical things, say he loved me, and that we would talk another day. But, the harder his life got, the less we talked. Sometimes weeks would go by and we wouldn't connect by phone. Living 400 miles apart meant I couldn't just jump in my car and go there whenever I pleased, and sometimes he didn't even want me to come. I took it as a normal, hard-working, busy man who didn't want mommy on his doorstep and so went to visit when invited. I thought it was the polite thing to do, but now realize he needed me more than he would allow himself to say. He was a self-sufficient man. I taught him to look after himself and very early on in life, he knew he could count on no one, not even me. I did the best I could, but it was difficult being mother, father, uncle, auntie, cousin, brother, sister, grandma, grandpa, and sometimes I just wanted time for me. In a normal family, that would be when grandma would babysit, so mom could just go and do and see, secure in the knowledge her child was at the best place he could be.

But my son's grandma was mentally ill, heard voices to kill us, hired people to harm us, and the very people we should have felt safe with, were the very people we had to run from.

I still foolishly believed we would be a success story. I still foolishly believed we were going to come out ahead, and someday our past would be just that; our past. Our future would be bright and happy and full of love and full of sunshine and full of people who loved us.

I foolishly believed...

Today was just a hang around day. I took the dog for a short walk and then had a long nap. I had checked out belly dancing classes and found out they were today.

Had met Jan from Canada the previous day and asked if she would be interested in going and she agreed. I picked up what I hoped would be a new friend and proceeded to the classes. Once there, the instructor said no, they weren't today, but another day next week. It was frustrating and whereas before I would have taken all this in stride, now I find little things not working out irritate me and add to a day already full of struggle. Struggle to wake up, struggle to smile, struggle to take step after step; why do more things not work out?

Jan and I went for a drink and I told her I had just lost my son but couldn't talk about it. We said all the niceties people who meet for the first time do, but even that was a struggle. After a few drinks, we both agreed it was time to go home and maybe meet another day. It's all a struggle and a chore and I still don't know how to fill the day.

So, I write and I write and I write.

And sometimes wonder who I'm writing for...

Day 23

I should have been a better mother. I should have been there for him more. When he withdrew, instead of being afraid he would push me away, I should have been in his face, in his space, and in his place.

I didn't know how to be a better mother. I thought love would be enough. And I loved him. I loved him so deeply, but didn't love him well. When he would come to me for advice, I would want so badly to say all the right things, but felt so inadequate and helpless in the wake of the suffering he had lived through. I didn't want to make a mistake in giving bad advice, for after all, he was the most precious person to ever walk this earth. I didn't want to steer him wrong, so many times steered him nowhere at all.

He had to grow up fast and wise. And he was wise. Many times I'd jokingly say, "Who raised you? Wolves?" It was my way of telling him he was so amazing, so smart, so giving, so loving and kind that no damaged human could have raised him up to be the fine man he became. For we are all damaged to one degree or another, and while some let the damage sink them, some overcome.

As said in practically every chapter written here, I sincerely thought we'd overcome.

This was too costly a mistake to make for he's not just away in another country. He's gone from this earth forever. And I don't want to stay.

What will I do? Probably nothing, for I'm not as brave as my son was. His friend said "That was the bravest, stupidest thing he'd ever done," and I agree.

Yesterday a friend from Canada asked if she could come visit me here in Mexico. I didn't realize, until I read her email, just how lonely I was. I quickly said yes and guaranteed I would make her transition here as easy as possible. This morning I woke up anxious to see if she'd sent an email saying she would indeed come. I also woke up with a feeling of apprehension that maybe she wouldn't. After dangling the proverbial carrot in front of this lonely rabbit, it would be very disappointing to have it snatched away.

We will see what comes of this for I no longer feel I deserve any smidgeon of kindness, any morsel of hope, or any glimmer of joy.

Today was a day spent alone, just my trusty perro and me. I had thought I was done with exploring, as I had braved the freeway, alligator jungle and seven mile deserted stretch of beach to the right of me, as well as successfully ascending and subsequently descending the rock bluff which brought me into civilization I was accustomed to and also running away from, to the left of me.

I had walked the avenida directly in front and found my crying ocean. All that was left was to climb the mountain behind. Today, that is what we did.

We climbed the broken cobblestone roadway, ever watchful for rooftop dogs and their counterparts down below. Some barked, some watched us, some left us alone. Kelly and I promptly reached our destination and were met with a panoramic view of the ocean to the one side of us. To the other side of the mountain top opened a view of the valley below, as yet undiscovered by us.

We meandered along the mountain pathways, no longer made of cobblestone, but now consisting of dirt, and then we meandered back. I stood on the mountaintop and gazed at the stretch of ocean below, hoping to inspire a sense of awe, a sense of beauty, or a sense of wonder at

God's handiwork. All I felt was anger and disappointment that my son would never be here to see this. All I felt was pain and sorrow that he no longer found this world a beautiful place to be, and that this world had brought him down.

Another mission accomplished, another conquest overcome, Kelly and I descended the steep mountain road and proceeded on to my crying ocean. At the time I did not realize today would be a crying day. I never know when the anguish will twist and turn and torment me to the point where I can hold back the tears no longer and have to let them flow.

The waves were the highest we've seen at the crying ocean, and I was hesitant to throw Kelly's stick very far. At one point, as she was searching for her prize, a gigantic wave arose, seemingly from nowhere, and pulled her under. She emerged shaking her head vigorously to remove the salty water from her ears. With an unsteady, wobbly walk, Kelly came out from her misadventure and was thereafter content to walk by my side, venturing no further.

We went as far as we could go on the one side of the sandy beach and then I stopped and watched the gargantuan waves. The more I watched the rhythm of the waves receding and advancing, the more I felt the rhythm of my heartbeat wanting to escape this pain.

As I have no manual for this, I am doing the best I can and trying the best I can to walk through each day. I know inside that each day I live is another day without my son, and the concept of facing a lifetime ahead without him continues to be a bottomless pit of despair.

I stood at the crying ocean and let my tears of hopelessness fall. Today I cried louder than I remember crying before, and I know a part of me wants to scream, but I kept looking around me for someone walking by. Have I really become so conscious of everyone else's comfort that, even in my grief, I worry about inconveniencing someone else if my sobbing is too loud? What is wrong with me?

I continued to cry and talked to my son. I told him how sorry I was for being a neglectful mother. I told him that many times I pushed him aside because he was so wonderful, and I was so not, that I didn't want to ruin him or wreck him or give him bad advice. I also told him that if he was ok, to let me know. I didn't want a butterfly, or a sweet saying, or anything that would make me imagine it was from him. I needed to know beyond a shadow of a doubt that it was my son letting me know he was fine.

Along with that request came the realization that it meant he was really gone. I know some part of me was still waiting for a phone call saying it was all a horrible mistake and someone else is buried where we thought we buried my son. I still want that call. I still want this to be a terrible mistake.

But, if I'm asking my son to show me he's ok wherever he is, then I must be realizing he is gone from this earth.

And that realization kills me inside...

Day 24

Know what bugs me? It bugs me when people say it's so lovely that I get to come to Mexico, and they envy me the sunshine and good times. It bugs me when people take a minuscule, meaningless event and try to make it so significant in my life.

Once again, my head and my heart are at war. My head understands they are trying to find some glimmer of hope for me to hold on to; my head understands they want to see a flicker of the "old Nina" come through. It's my heart. My heart is broken and feels offended when the sorrow of all sorrows can be somehow minimized even to a slight degree. My heart is angry, although the anger still hasn't arisen, and somehow I feel more than fifty years of anger has to surface before I can even begin to heal.

That anger has been buried and subdued for most of my life, and I do wonder what is there, seething below the surface of the nice person I thought I'd become. There was so much injustice done to us, and instead of reacting and defending us, I lay down like a cowering, whimpering puppy that was being beaten. Even when I was no longer being beaten, I continued to lay there, helpless and unable to rise. I thought by lying in one spot and causing no waves, the world would leave me alone. I thought by lying there and never fighting back, eventually the world would see and understand that I was no threat to anyone and could be molded at anyone's command. I thought by raising my child to never fight back and to be true to yourself in knowing you cause no one any pain, would somehow reward him with a big payoff at the end.

Dear God, help me to forgive myself, for I thought so wrong.

What does it matter now to think right, even if I knew how?

We do the best we can, hoping for the best we can, and no parent ever imagines the outcome I've had.

No parent imagines their child is that unhappy and unfulfilled that they would choose death over life.

No parent ever imagines watching their child be put in the ground.

No parent should ever have to imagine any of these occurrences.

And no parent should ever have to feel this pain.

Today I awoke to a cloudy day. It is the first day that isn't scorching hot and was a bit of a surprise, for you become accustomed to your surroundings very quickly, and take for granted the weather will always be as it has been for the past twenty-three days. My wardrobe of choice for the day will have to be rethought and revised.

I made plans with Barb today. She and I had met last Friday when I sang my infamous Karaoke songs, which still leaves me with a feeling of accomplishment. I wonder what today will bring.

It is the American Thanksgiving and since I'm Canadian, has no relevance to me, but the Mexican people have deemed it a day worthy to celebrate in honor of their American tourists. Barb and I bought tickets for dinner and drinks and will be going over to Rincon de Guayabitos later in the day.

Before, I would look forward to anything even remotely pertaining to fun, but now am hesitant, worried and apprehensive wondering if I can make it through the day without crying. While everyone says, "If you cry, you cry, people have to understand," they're also not the ones sitting crying at the dinner table. I watch others discomfort when my tears flow and therefore prefer to do it alone.

Hence the conundrum. As few see me cry, I am then told how much better I'm doing and how lucky I am to be in Mexico and how envious everyone is of me and my great adventure, which brings me back to my original sentence of today, Day 24 in Mexico, grieving my son.

While we are all doing the best we can in a situation that never should have been, I do so sincerely wish people would be cautious in envying anything good that might come to us grieving parents, for, truth be told, we are barely hanging on.

Day 25

Today I am sick. My chest hurts, I'm coughing and I'm cold. I woke up in the night, unable to get warm and feeling very ill in Mexico.

I'd received an email from the two women from Nova Scotia with whom I'd gone to Karaoke the Friday before. They wanted to tell me they'd arrived home safely and what a pleasure it was to meet me. They said of all the people they'd met during their Mexican vacation I was their favorite and definitely stood out from the crowd.

While it could just be flowery words they say to everyone, I'd been told that before, that I stand out from the crowd, and I'm the nicest, the funniest, the one people most remember. So, it would appear my lifelong quest to be accepted and liked had worked, and people drew to me; people who had their own families and children and husbands and hope for tomorrow and happiness for today.

I know their words were meant to make me feel better and another time, they might have. Now, I only felt more despondency than ever before. For what good was it if the whole world loved me and yet I no longer had my child? What good was any of it and what good can come of it now? My child is gone. He's gone.

Because I'm in a country my son and I had never been to together, sometimes I forget he's gone and feel as though I'm just away for awhile and will see him when I'm back. During those times I act normal and actually laugh and no one would know the inner turmoil inside. During those times, I voraciously gulp laughter as though it were air. During those times, I get a reprieve from the pain.

The next day I crash and burn and whereas yesterday I was so high I felt I could fly, today I'm so low I have to look up to see bottom. This is a roller coaster ride and others tell me the times in between the lows will get further and further apart. I don't know as I haven't experienced that yet, but do realize that, for now, when I laugh, I feel disrespectful to my son. I feel as though I am not grieving him enough and when I hear of mothers who have lost children say they were a complete zombie for the first year, I wonder what is so callous in me that I'm not a zombie. Oh, I do strange things and I don't concentrate and am very sensitive and have a difficult time making small talk, but sometimes, here in Mexico, I dance and I laugh and I twirl and twirl and twirl until I twirl away the pain. And then, without warning, I see my little boy's face, and chide myself for even entertaining the thought of ever being happy again.

So, I sit, alone in Mexico, feeling more alone than I've ever felt before, and know this is my life, and doubt I will do much to change it.

Today I am sick, and know there is much more to say, but feel too weak to continue, so will write more another day...

Day 26

What's worse than being alone in Mexico? Being alone and sick in Mexico. I feel so weak that making a cup of tea is an effort, and wonder how it is I came to be this alone in a world with so many people.

The only thing I can come up with is I deserve this.

I deserve to be alone and lonely and sick and unhappy and to have my child gone. I no longer know what my religious beliefs are but Buddhists apparently believe you pay in this life for all the wrong you did in the past one. While I always thought that was very unfair of God to punish you for something you didn't even remember doing, I also think it's very unfair of God to hear my prayers for my son, and turn away.

I don't know what else to say, except accepting that I deserve this and knowing I should never again try to find any peace or happiness in this world almost gives me a false sense of calm. It also makes me sad because I believe I had a lot to offer this world, but then so did my son. We both didn't make it, and now, here I sit, alone in Mexico, feeling so sick I secretly want to get sicker and die.

Who would find me? Who would care? Who would mourn me much longer after I was gone?

It would be a fitting end to a fitting tumultuous life. We now are just statistics; the end justified the means. They lived a harrowing, heartbreaking life, the son took his own life, the mother is as the walking dead, and eventually died in a room in a fishing village in Mexico. That is as it should be.

Who were they that thought they might escape? Who were they that thought they would bring about joy in their lives? Who were they to go against the gods who, obviously long ago, predicted their fate and decided they would not survive? Who were they who searched for love? Who were they who crumbled when they didn't find it? Who were they to believe in a fairytale ending? Who were they who wanted to overcome?

They were misinformed as to the rules of life, and should have accepted long ago they couldn't win.

The mother knows it now and will be careful and cautious to never try again.

I've learnt my lesson well, and there is nothing more you could take from me to teach me I don't deserve a rich, fulfilling life.

I will never try again, I will never hope again, I will never believe again, I will never love again.

For now that you took my son, I have no one to love...

Day 27

Periodically, I wake up throughout the night full of thoughts, fragments of dreams, or just musings in my mind and then know what it is I will write about the next morning. Last night, even though I had taken my nightly cocktail of sleeping meds, herbal relaxants and whatever else I've needed to get me through each night since the passing of my son, sleep still eluded me and found me struggling to sink into that welcome abyss.

I rarely have felt anger in my life and while others say that is an admirable quality, I feel it is a deep flaw within. For when I should have been angry at injustices done to my son and myself, I instead curled deep within myself, covered my hands over my head, and cowered and quivered in fear. It would be as though I were paralyzed, unable to speak, unable to move, unable to think, and worst of all, unable to feel. I would let whatever excruciatingly terrifying circumstance happen to us, just happen, and would make light of it to my son, in hopes he too, could somehow become paralyzed or invisible, so nothing more could hurt him.

He wasn't as good an actor as I was and, in the end, could no longer hold it in.

I still do, and sometimes wonder what is wrong with me that I can laugh so soon after he's gone. I sometimes can't hear or even write his name almost as if that means he's not really gone. Or maybe because it's too painful to bear and I lived through too many painful to bear moments, so can't conceive dealing with the most painful of all. When the grief attacks, I curl deep inside, cover my hands over my head and cower and quiver in fear. I am hoping to paralyze the residual feelings of love and yearning and longing I still hold inside.

With the fight to close down all emotions, anger somehow got trapped in the cyclone swirling high above, and never did land on me again.

Even now, I find it perplexing that I'm angry at so little. I don't feel the rage others talk about and I don't feel the rage I think I should feel. I'm afraid.

I'm afraid, if the anger is unleashed, to discover how much of it is there.

I'm also afraid I won't know what to do with it and it will take me down.

And now I have no one who will care for me.

For I truly am alone in this world.

Alone and sick in Mexico...

However, this was not how this chapter was going to end. Throughout my sleepless night, I felt angry at the doctors back in Canada. Doctors who knew I was sick with lung problems and yet chose to do nothing, all the while dismissing my feeble complaints as just that. I felt angry that I had gone for a routine scope down the throat to see into my gall bladder, awoke during the procedure, and felt the surgeon tear the scope from within. I felt angry that the first thought, after their mistake, was for the negligent nurse to realize I hadn't signed the consent form for the surgery, and for them to quickly rectify that situation while I writhed in agony. I felt angry that the surgeon had cut my pancreas and I was fighting for my life with the torturous pain ripping me apart. I felt angry that they had done damage to my lungs to where I didn't breath for years without gasping for air. I felt angry that I suffered, these seven years, with ill health, difficulty breathing, clammy, cold skin, struggling to breathe, and continually living with the feeling a ton of cement has been dropped on my chest.

I felt angry that I just accepted it as my due and learned to live with it the best way I knew how. How does one human being get so beaten down she won't stand for herself at all? How does a human being get so beaten down she won't even feel anger towards those who have caused her harm? How does a human being allow any atrocity to be done to her and fights back not at all?

It starts with being raised in a family full of hate, other than a dad who also was full of fear, and ends with her son taking his life?

Now, I matter even less to me, for whatever fight I had in me, I tried to let it be for him. He's gone so what matters what this world does to me now?

And yet, this is when the anger has begun. Too little, too late, I say. I should have fought harder for my child and maybe he would still be here today. When I see how vicious, greedy and selfish my brothers are, I turn away and want to be nothing like them. And yet they succeeded in their life and their selfishness brought them great gain. In this world that would be the key to success. Fight, claw, kick, walk over whoever you can, and you will be greatly rewarded. Don't tell me they'll get theirs in the next world. I'm not in the next world, I'm in this one. And this is all I know. And truth be told, this is all you know, too. You can only speculate.

And I believe I so badly wanted to be loved that I created a God of love who would watch over us and protect us. And I think sometimes weak people want revenge, so they create a God of vengeance, saying they'll get theirs. What a stupid saying. Because if that's true, my son and I, we sure got ours, didn't we?

Punishable by death...

But, God, what was our crime?

After a restless, fitful, sleepless night, Kelly the dog and I were awakened by loud banging on our door and the melodious voice of my neighbor, Sharon. She and my other new neighbor, Marilyn, whom I haven't had an opportunity to introduce you to yet, had come to take my dog for her morning walk.

I was so touched by the kindness of these two virtual strangers I started to cry. The tears flowed, unabated, and I felt more cared about than I have for a long time at home. Maybe I'm in the wrong home.

The dog walkers will be back at two...

Day 28

Today proved to be no better a day than yesterday, and I do find myself questioning the purpose of anger. Is it an emotion meant to spur you on to perhaps achieve a better consequence than the one you may have humbly taken, never having felt the anger within? Is it meant to torment you further than you already are tormented by the circumstance that may have brought about the anger? Or is it meant to take your mind off the hardships of the day?

No matter. It is a new and unusual emotion for me to be feeling and it would appear the sickness throughout my body, and the sense of injustice it has brought about, has left me agitated and irritated all day long.

It started with last night my telling the wonderful dog walkers that I would set my alarm and be awake and alert when they came to get the dog, as I sincerely appreciated the task they had undertaken. No worries, I was assured, sleep as long as you like. We'll be by when we're by.

I'd already advised my new friends that the doctor I had an appointment with today had said not to come till late afternoon, so knew it need not be an early morning.

With another sleep deprived night spent tossing and turning, only to awaken fitfully coughing with my throat raw and dry, around 4:00 a.m. I finally succumbed to taking more sleeping aids, secure that I wouldn't be awakened early in the morn.

Still under the effects of a drug induced slumber, I was startled by persistent banging at eight in the morning. Bright eyed and cheery, there were my neighbors come to take the dog, all the while informing me our other neighbor, who had a car, would be driving us to the doctor appointment and to be ready by nine.

Groggy and disoriented, I tried to explain the doctor wouldn't be there as he quite avidly informed me not to come before the late afternoon. My paltry pleadings were met with resistance, so unshowered and uncoiffed, I found myself in the front seat of the car, speeding towards what we hoped was the doctor's open door.

Upon arrival, it was evident no doctor was present, and as we sat in the hot car, adding to my discomfort, waiting for him to open his doors, my new driver proceeded to tell an interminable, monotonous story of how she didn't get along with her brother-in-law and all his shortcomings as a man.

Relating to a caged animal, willing to take any means of escape, I looked for the nearest speeding vehicle to come careening around the corner, having full intentions of throwing myself under its wheels.

My discomfort was very obvious to all and with the sweltering heat, lack of ventilation, continuous drone of a voice I was desperately trying to drown out, I thought I would expire, right there on the doorstep of the recalcitrant doctor; the one who had already told me not to come before late afternoon.

Suffering the interminable monologue as much as I could bear, I finally pleaded with my captives to take me home and set me free. We would try again in the afternoon.

Sleepless, sapless, helpless, hopeless, morose, fatigued and very ill, the day continued to annoy and irritate me.

What is all the hype about letting your anger out? For where do you let it out when no one is to blame? Where do you direct your anger when you don't even know who is at fault for your life?

You direct it at you, for in reality, you are the only one you have even a smidgeon of hope to control.

I am learning a lot about myself in these writings but unfortunately it is too late to help my son. Don't tell me it's not too late to help myself for I don't deserve to be helped. I let my child die, and did nothing to save him.

Throughout the past two nights, while suffering with my malady, I've had a sense I could let go and die. As the doctor said I have a fever and am quite ill, I don't know if these are delusions or not, but the one night I felt my body, feet firmly planted on the floor, reach up to the sky. There was a light up above me as I was in a room of darkness and could see nothing else. I sensed that if I pulled up towards the light I could go; the choice was mine to make. Something deep inside me, something I've never known existed and have never explored, had a knowing that I could pull up and my body would release and die. My feet felt very heavy and they were holding me firmly on this earth, while my inner makings, or soul, if you will, knew it would fly.

I became afraid and for only a moment wanted to go. Then, I thought it isn't that I want to die; it's that I want my son to live and have another chance at happiness. I had another chance at happiness the winter in Arizona before he died. And with the inner joy I felt, my countenance changed so noticeably that friends who came to visit from home, were amazed at the transformation in me. With this change came renewed hope for a better future for my son and I, and I looked forward to seeing him again so we could begin anew. Neither of us got that chance for before I came home, he was gone.

Why?

Why?

Why?

I need him to be here, just to try again. Just to try one more time and maybe this time, he and I, we'll succeed, and we'll be happy, and we'll find love, and we'll find joy, and we'll realize all the things that were so unimportant in life, and be able to let them go.

I just want one more try.

I don't know how to stop being a mother.

And don't tell me I still am, because I'm not.

See, the anger is there. Let it come, I say. If my son could see me he'd probably agree. The only problem is I do remember feeling anger. It was always directed at him, for he was safe and would still love me no matter what. That was why I stopped being angry and began to hold it in. Sadly, I also held in so many other emotions that he needed to know.

There is no one else in the world I have ever been secure and comfortable enough with to say loved me with no conditions. Maybe it's my perception or maybe it's the fact of my life, but after all, our life is really how we perceive it and maybe not how it is at all. Our perception of our life is our reality and we make our foibles and foolish decisions because of it.

The doctor told my friend I am dangerously ill. He said to call anytime, night or day. I don't have oxygen going to my brain and am light headed, dizzy, stumble when I try to walk, and disoriented.

I don't know if that's attributed to the night thinking I could maybe die, but I will let you come to your own conclusion. I believe it was real.

Once I knew I didn't really want to die, I pulled back from the light and felt my feet plant firmer on this earth. Once again I let fear dictate my life and pulled back from something that may have drawn me closer to my son.

Strangely enough, I thought of this book, and wondered who would finish if I were to go?

Day 29

Just another gnarly day in paradise, and I am the gnarly queen.

There's an old Jewish saying that goes something like this: A father was at the bottom of the stairs, encouraging his son to jump. "Jump," he said to the son, "and I will catch you." The son jumped and when the father caught him, the son was filled with love. When the father didn't catch him, the son was filled with something else. He was filled with "life".

I just want you to know, God, that I've had enough of the "life" moments. I've had enough of the moments where you didn't catch me. I've had enough experiences that show me life isn't fair, and duly-noted, God, I hold "life" in the lowest esteem.

Especially today.

I am sick, have difficulty breathing, am immersed in pain, and it's no longer just emotional and mental, but now we have added the physical. I don't know where to run from myself and the mess I've made of this gift you call life. I have tried to the best of my ability to cherish this gift and treat it wisely and fair. We've already had the discussion where I've realized I've failed, for I failed at the most important job I was given. I failed to watch over the greatest gift I received; the gift of a child.

I remember when my son was five years old and I had a recurring dream which would not go away. In the dream I was holding on tightly to my son, for I was so afraid of my family and the abuse they had brought upon us. We were in hiding, we were running, and I feared, not only for my child's safety, but for his peace of mind. For I knew the horrors he had seen in such a young life, and I clung on tightly, afraid to let him go.

In my dream I saw Jesus reach out His arms towards my son and ask me to give my child to Him. Desperately holding onto my child, for if I didn't protect him, who would, I refused to give him up. Jesus continued to look into my eyes and again asked for me to willingly give him up. Finally relenting, I handed my child over to Jesus and released him from my arms. Jesus took my son into his arms, hugged him, and handed him back to me. I knew then that my son belonged to God first and me second and throughout the years, reminded God of that dream and would ask that my son be protected, blessed and loved. I thought God had given my son back to me and I would never have to give him up again.

I didn't think you would take him, God. I didn't think you meant he was more yours than he was mine. I thought I would grow old watching my son fulfill his dreams for he had many dreams and worked so hard. He never asked for anyone to help him but tirelessly worked towards achieving the hopes he nurtured inside. Why did you take him, God? Why couldn't there have been a different outcome? Why couldn't my child have outlived me?

I haven't cried for many days, and yet, as I'm writing this, I am crying. I am sick and crying and alone and lonely in Mexico.

And I feel like a trained seal, writing my chapter a day. It's as though this is my purpose and my destiny and I am to continue to write my chapter a day. I feel as though I've been shackled and brought down so low, I dare not resist what I've been put on this earth to do. Deep inside, I always knew I was to write, and have been told by many that I draw the reader in. Whether this is true or not remains to be seen, but I do know my words take flight, as if they have a will of their own, and many times I write what I had no intention of saying.

For I know, like the trained seal I am, that the light of day will not pass before I've completed my chapter. So, wanting to do the best job I can, I ponder my day's activities, thoughts, writings, musings and diatribes, and come up with all form of interesting, insightful things to say. But, when I sit poised over my computer, fingers flexed to begin, the words that come forth are rarely what I have concluded to write throughout the day.

These words have a life of their own. And sometimes they continue on and sometimes they inadvertently stop and I no longer know what to say.

Today is one of those days where I want the words to stop, for I am holding in emotion that is seething, wrestling, fighting it's way to the forefront of my mind, and I am dizzy with knowing I am holding so much in. If I stop the words, then I can do what I've always done, and have become so proficient at doing. I can move, shove, hold down the feelings and continue on with my day, no one being the wiser, no one knowing I am a cauldron of indescribable pain, that one day will surface and I will cease to exist as I am. I will cease to be the finely honed instrument of politeness and poise I have manufactured myself into. I will cease to be the one who worries more about others than she does about herself. I will cease to be the person who puts aside her hopes, her dreams, her ambitions, her search for a place to belong, her quest to be loved. I will put her aside and perhaps, just perhaps, become the person I was always meant to be.

But, at what cost?

Did my son have to die so I could finally live?

No, no, no, no. I'm screaming inside, "Nooooooooo," and don't even know where that thought came from. I want to erase those words for they make me a monster. But, I can't erase those words, for I do wonder if throughout his short life, I worried so much about his safety that I ceased to exist.

I just ceased to exist.

And I am the selfish, fallible, broken human who is destined to stay on this selfish, fallible, broken world, while I know my son was too good to stay.

Even as I'm writing this, I can sense scoffers and sceptics say, "She is making her son out to be some perfect person, with no flaws of his own."

No.

He was just a far better person than you or I...

Day 30

Remember the friend I'd mentioned might come to visit, some chapters ago? Well, we were communicating back and forth and I was telling her I was quite ill, but tried to help where I could. She politely informed me she could manage to find her own way here and I needn't concern myself with helping her too much.

She also informed me she would stay with me until she worked things out. That would not work for me. Firstly, I'm in mourning and my sleep routine is very unpredictable. Secondly, my place is too small for two people to live in comfortably, and thirdly, I'm sick. These were in no way reflections of our friendship or of her at all. These were just my circumstances and whereas, before, I would have made do and made myself uncomfortable and tried too hard to please, if this horrid experience has taught me anything, it has taught me I need to learn to speak up and say when something doesn't work for me.

I realized I never spoke up before because I didn't want to inconvenience anyone else and chose rather to put my own needs aside. I also didn't want people to leave me and wanted them to stay around me, no matter the cost to self. It didn't matter if you were a good friend, an indifferent friend, or a bad one; I wanted them all. I just wanted to be surrounded by anyone and everyone and would do all that was within my power, and sometimes beyond, not to be alone.

How then, did I end up so alone, feeling I belong nowhere with no one?

For, when I told this friend the apartment below me was being held for her but was only available for three weeks she sent me an email today saying she wouldn't be coming after all, for she had wanted to stay a few months and vacation for the winter.

Nowhere had we discussed her staying many months and I sincerely hoped she had not planned to stay with me those months. But then what had I ever done in the past to make someone think they couldn't? Nothing. It would make sense that anyone who knew me before would find moving in utterly acceptable as telling me what they were going to do was not unusual at all.

And while I still don't want to be as alone and lonely in Mexico as I am, it made me angry. I know part of my anger stems from the fact that I am so unwell, part of the anger stems from the fact that I used to walk off my frustration and now am unable to do so, and part of the anger stems from the fact I no longer have anything to lose and realize I hung onto people that really were not worth hanging on to. I'm not saying this is the case with this friend, I am just generalizing.

The first thing I did was send her an email back saying I was very confused and what had changed, as I had never been told all her wishes. Then, I got angrier still and wrote her another email saying her decision had not only confused me, it had hurt me, and this was a terrible way to treat me.

Com'n world, this is a terrible way to treat me!

But how would you know if I never say anything or show you what's acceptable and what's not? How can I fault you, world, when I've just laid down like a little puppy dog, aching to be petted and surprised when I was kicked? How can I fault you, world, when having been kicked, I continued to lick your hand and hoped next time would be different?

The next time was never different and I'm sitting here wondering what to do with this anger. I don't want to write anymore. I don't know how to express anger and don't know what to do with it. I want to go for a long, long walk, but am unable to breathe without feeling faint, wobble when I walk, and am so weak I barely can stand.

I know I'm sick. I know I'm very, very sick.

And I'm tired. So tired.

But I don't want to leave this world thinking my life was of no purpose. For you see, my purpose was my son.

And now, he's gone...

So, today my chapter was going to end here, but I stopped writing feeling restless and unfulfilled. Usually when I'm done the chapter, I feel a sense of accomplishment, a sense of rightness, a sense that I had just done what I was supposed to do. Today I wrote only out of a sense of duty to write my chapter a day.

Yesterday's revelation scared me and it was difficult admitting my dark thoughts and dark feelings, but if I'm going to write this, I have to be open and honest, especially with myself. And my thoughts right now are dark and I see no light and I see no sense of joy.

I know my friend not coming is probably the right thing. I know I would try to entertain her, even while she would be saying I didn't need to. I know me, and I know I still would. And that is not why I'm here. I'm not sure why I'm here, but do think it's to write this book and also to grieve. Neither of these things would be accomplished if I had someone here a great deal of the time.

So, while I want to run away into fun and merriment and be like the rest of the vacationer's here, I also know I can't carry around this amount of pretense anymore.

After writing what I thought was an acceptable number of words, and feeling the frustration, I couldn't find a place for myself. I wanted to kick, scream, run, yell but had no energy to do any of those things. A friend had sent me a cute saying about how God sends things to comfort us and we turn away from them, then wonder why He doesn't comfort. Usually I ask people to stop sending me emails like this and many times delete them without even looking. This time I opened up the cute saying, thought it was exactly that, and noticed there was music. My sound hadn't been working on my computer and it was just another frustration to me that things don't seem to work right. This time I searched for a way to correct the problem and was successful. Happy with that outcome, I listened to the song on my inspirational email and it did what it was meant to do. It soothed.

I wanted the feeling to continue so went looking for more inspirational songs on the internet. And then, more and more. And I let them play throughout the building, with my door open, because maybe there were others today that needed to be inspired, too.

While I struggle with anger, I sense my son always saying for me to forgive. I know I have to forgive everyone who has slighted me and hurt him, although now it is difficult for me to do.

I also know I'll eventually forgive my friend, but for now, I will leave things as they are. There's a scripture that says, "Let your yes be yes and your no be no", and people in grief need things to be clear.

We are expending all of our energy in our grief, and can't take on any other complications or difficulties. So, before you commit to us, make sure you will try and follow through. We still understand that life happens and circumstances change, but don't throw us a lifesaver as we're sinking, and then whisk it away, with no explanation or seeming remorse.

For you see, world, my house is burning down all around me. Quit fanning the embers and throwing more logs on the flames.

Day 31

I am so ill my mind doesn't seem to work right. I say things I don't mean and sometimes, in my quest for laughter, try and make a joke, but it is never funny. Others look at me perplexed and where once they would have laughed and commended my dry, witty sense of humor, now they only stare. I wonder if it's the grief that makes me so different, or if it's the inflection of my voice that no longer amuses?

I don't know how to be this new person without her son. I don't know how to be her, and I don't want to be her. I had a hard enough time liking the one I was before and now that all my defenses are down, all my personas have been stripped away, all that I tried to be was found wanting, I don't know how to be.

I just don't know how to be.

I second guess everything I say and don't want any more losses, so look quickly at everyone's face to make sure they still want to be around me. I want to cry more than I do, and I want my friends to comfort me, but I don't want to bring them down when they're having a happy day.

I don't know who to be anymore.

I sit alone in Mexico wondering where everyone is, wondering how it was I didn't succeed in my mission to dazzle the multitudes and be surrounded by those who care. Some say, now that I'm sick, to come home, but I don't know where home is. I never felt safe or secure in a physical home and my home was always where my son was.

When he died, I wanted to save his house so I could move in. I understood how he didn't want to give the house up for it was probably the only home he'd ever really known.

It was also the only home I ever wanted to know, for I felt a misfit everywhere else, sometimes even with him.

I felt we were branded unlovable and strived so hard to change that perception.

When I was looking for a place for Kelly the dog and I to live here in Mexico, I was dealing with a real estate lady and she assured me the landlords would have no trouble with me bringing a small dog. I advised her that the dog was not small and rather, quite large, and left it at that.

Some time went by before we were in contact again, at which point I'd been dealing with the landlady to whom English was a second language. I'm sure I did mention the dog, as it would have been impossible to keep a secret, but am still not sure whether or not the size of the dog was understood.

When I arrived, exhausted and worn out from the long day's sojourn, the landlady commented on the size of the dog and that, for some reason, she thought I was bringing a small one. Quickly I reassured her it was a very good dog and hoped Kelly would not prove me wrong.

Today the landlady petted my dog and said how very sweet she was and I was instantly reassured we could stay. The landlord had already given his approval some weeks back, so it was comforting to know that now the landlady concurred. I told Kelly she was a good girl, and then realized how much I wanted her to behave so we would not have to look for another place to live.

I realized I'd done that with my son many times, and always wanted him to behave and be good and not cause any waves. I wanted the whole world to let us stay.

I do understand I'll never know all the circumstances of why my son had to leave, but I do know I fault myself at every turn. How do I stop? I don't know.

For I was the mother, I should have protected him more.

I may stop writing for a few days until I get this lung infection under control. For I sense I am going round and round in circles and don't even remember if I've already written the words I'm writing today. I have a fever and feel very sad and alone. I feel so sad I wish there was somewhere to escape to. But I can't escape this feeling of sadness, so I sit in it, enveloped like a blanket. Except this blanket gives no warmth; it gives no comfort; it does not snuggle around me and make me feel safe and protected. This blanket is harsh and made of barbs and cuts wherever it falls. This blanket is with me always. It has now covered my soul.

Day 32

Do you know what I want? I want somewhere where I can be grumpy and still have the person care and love me. I realize the only place I had that was with my son. I have to honestly say I don't think he had that with me. I couldn't bear him being sad and when I would see him sad, it tore me in two. I also think the unspoken speaks louder than the spoken and he would have known that without being told.

So, he held everything in, and he, too, had nowhere to be grumpy and still feel loved.

My only immediate family consists of an aunt, an uncle, two cousins and their spouses. When my son died, my aunt was at the funeral, but then, I hardly heard from her for three months. It was devastation upon devastation and I had nothing within me to reach out, so I waited and I waited and finally she reached out to me.

As we were having our conversation, she let me know she hadn't been in touch because I'd snapped at her at the funeral. I'd snapped at her at the funeral? I don't even remember what I said or who I was or who was there or what I ate or when I slept, but the paramount thing, world, was I needed to watch my tongue.

Then, one of my closest friends, who I used to hear from every day, did the same. She just disappeared from my life, M.I.A., not to be heard from. Mutual friends told me to contact her, as we had been so close, and I said, no, I would wait for her to contact me. She finally did and then told me it looked like I had a lot of friends around me and she felt snubbed by me at the funeral, so backed away. Snubbed by me at the funeral?

Is this really the love I have surrounding me?

Did I always know that?

Or is this just normal?

And I'm searching for something that doesn't exist?

So yesterday my neighbor commented how grumpy her husband was when he was sick a few weeks ago. It was all good natured kidding and you could see she was over it as soon as it happened. The thing that stood out most for me was that he had the freedom to be grumpy because he was after all sick, and when you're sick, you're grumpy, but he knew after he got well, she would still be there to care.

I fear being grumpy because I don't know if anyone will be there to care. In the past, other than my son, no one was. And his passing showed me many people care, and I am blessed for the friends and family who stood by me, but I need and want somewhere where I'm not holding in my emotions and can let the tears flow, knowing someone will be there to hold me after.

Sitting here, alone and lonely and sick in Mexico, I don't have that. For some reason, I felt I had that even less back home. Is my loneliness only a frame of mind because the one I loved the most is gone. Are my thoughts all misconstrued and wonky because of my illness? Do I, just for today, feel so lost and alone, but in a few hours, when I get an encouraging email, be flying high? Well, as high as a person can fly, given my circumstances.

Day 33

Do you ever get the feeling you're not living the life you were meant to live? That somewhere you zigged where you should have zagged and your entire life took a wrong direction? Do you ever get the feeling you're on your own to figure it out and any illusions or misconceptions you may have had that anyone else is along for the ride, were wrong?

Oh, they may hitch on to your coattails for a brief period of time, usually solely based on your ability to provide an amusement factor, but in reality, you're on your own.

Even God. By now I should probably stop picking on God, but I have no one else to pick on and I figure He's God, He can take it.

I did try briefly, through this saddest of all sad, and in my desperation to quell the ache inside any way I could, to see counsellors. That was met with disastrous results and I came to realize it is very broken people trying hard to fix more broken people. Like dominoes we all go down. The only saving grace for the counsellors, however, is they have credentials and their delusions about their own importance behind them. We, the hurting, have no defense, and if we are one of the fortunate few who get a kind, understanding counsellor, we are the better for it.

I was not that lucky. I had kind people who came in and out of my life in the form of hospice workers and the like. They are to be highly commended for the work they do, but, in all honesty, I needed to talk to someone who had gone through similar to what I'd gone through. First I had to try a whole bunch of "wrongs" before I found who I thought was a "right" fit as a counsellor.

Since I sat zombie like, unable to boil water to make a cup of tea, my friend found a bible based, grief support counsellor for me. I went to see him and could tell right away we didn't click. He tried so very hard to be a compassionate, listening ear that I didn't have the heart to tell him this wasn't working. I think it started with him reading me the scripture verses where King David had sinned against God by orchestrating the murder of a man married to the woman King David lusted after. Once the man was dead, King David did indeed marry the object of his affection, Bathsheba, and they produced a son. According to the bible, King David thought he got away with the crime, but God brought forth punishment, and the son died. Until the son's death, King David sat and prayed and beseeched God to be merciful, but upon hearing the son was gone, King David picked himself up, brushed himself off, and started writing psalms to God agreeing he had to pay for his sin and was indeed a wicked man.

When this counsellor started reading the psalms where David expounded the magnitude of his sin, I sat there incredulous, looked at the counsellor, and said, "But, what exactly is my sin? And what are you trying to say? That now that my son is gone, I should just pick myself up, brush myself off, and say, thanks for playing, God. You win, I lose, my son paid."

This counsellor agreed maybe I didn't fit into this scenario, and we moved on.

Next time I opened up and shared my anger at God for having allowed my son to go. The counsellor, quite seriously, looked at me and said, "You are hurting God by your anger", to which I inwardly responded, "God can handle it." Outwardly, I looked around for the hidden camera, because surely this was a joke, shook the counsellor's hand, thanked him for his time, and left, never to return.

Now I was sans counsellor, and many friends, in their concern and helplessness, encouraged me to find another. One friend even went so far as to say she couldn't remain my friend because of my stubbornness to get into counselling immediately. She has not returned and I miss her for we had been friends a long time.

Since I drove all the way from Tucson, Arizona to Calgary, Alberta once I heard of my son's death, I know I was in shock the entire drive, and stopped at hospitals along the way. I couldn't even tell you for sure which hospitals I stopped at, although I would believe them over me. I was in a daze.

Upon returning home, the hospital bills started coming in to the tune of thousands of dollars and while I had medical coverage that would reimburse me, I didn't have the wherewithal to fill out the forms or even to pay. People were coming and going to my house and one friend would start the process, only to have to leave, and the next one would struggle as to where one left off and she was to begin. It was as if my brain was on sabbatical and what would have been such a simple task before was now insurmountable. In my helplessness, I phoned the hospitals telling them what happened and to please be patient. I was not ignoring the bills, just give me some time. I documented the calls, dates, and times, and sometimes would appear quite lucid and organized, while other times not. One friend did say it was confusing because I presented well. She said it would seem I understood everything that was being said, and then, in one sentence from me, they could see nothing had penetrated and I was lost as to what anyone was saying.

If someone spoke more than a few words of direction, I couldn't comprehend and when I would ask a question, I asked for please only a "yes" or a "no", for if I got an explanation, my eyes would swim before me, and I had no grasp of what was said.

These hospitals in the U.S., while agreeing they would wait, didn't wait, and proceeded to send me to collections. The collection agencies were relentless in their pursuit and I was floundering, trying to understand everything that was going on.

Throughout this ordeal, one place I was extremely blessed was with my family doctor. She was new and the first time she met me was shortly after I arrived back in British Columbia. She was very kind and I cannot say enough about her. I hope someday she reads this, and I would like to say more about this wonderful doctor, but as this is not about her, I have to move on.

Feeling so defeated, I turned to her, and explained the collection agency/hospital situation. She, in turn, found a counsellor who, while it wasn't his job, agreed to help me with some of the pressing matters that couldn't be put on hold; this situation being one of them.

When I met him, I told him my frustration and how, when I lived in the same world my son lived in, I would be the one to sort out matters like this for others. Now it was incredibly frustrating to not even be able to comprehend the simplest of tasks. I would look at the phone and not understand how to dial. I would look at a bill and start to shake for I didn't remember how to respond. I had to make big decisions as to my son's affairs, and wanted to tell everyone he would be back and then he could decide, for he was only away working and surely he would return. Please don't do anything with his house or his things; just leave everything as it is. He will be back. He just has to be.

Compounded upon the decisions for him were the decisions for me, and I wished there was someone to help.

When this counsellor offered to help, I was thankful and opened up about all I was dealing with and that there was only me to do it. Friends tried to help, but in the end, it was still only me to make the final decisions.

When this counsellor told me he had lost a son to cancer some years back, I instantly bonded and felt a kinship to him. Sometimes we would discuss prevalent matters such as these hospital bills and sometimes I would pour out my heart and felt the freedom to cry when I cried, laugh when I laughed, and talk when I talked. I thought we shared a common bond.

I was wrong.

Purely by happenstance, I ended up with the report this counsellor wrote about me. Feeling confident it would be kind and compassionate, I opened it and began to read. It hurts me still that this counsellor twisted what I said and painted me in such a bad light. He literally ripped me apart. Now, scoffers would say many don't like their counsellors and so maybe I'm overreacting in my grief. While what was said in his office will forever remain a case of he said, she said, this counsellor and I emailed privately and there, he contradicts himself.

In the emails he states how funny I am and how many times he would read what I said and burst out laughing. In his report he says I viciously attacked him verbally and he doesn't think it's my grief, but rather who I always was as a person. When I read the report to my friend, she asked who he was writing about, and when I said it was me, she stated it's so far from who you are, it's almost laughable.

I told this counsellor I read his report and he, at least, had the decency to look embarrassed. His face went red, and instantly defensive, he wanted to know where I got it. I told him that was irrelevant and wasn't it my file, after all? Still very defensive, he said I needed to go through the proper channels, which was the Freedom of Information Act, where they would black out what he didn't want me to see.

I knew further talking to this cruel, insecure little man would be of no value, so sat there quietly, now too afraid to speak. After some moments of silence, he said, "Well, you certainly are calm considering what you just read." He knew, too, that he had written slanderous remarks and was very unkind. I told him, "My legs are completely numb. That is how this report shocked me." We said our goodbyes and his last remark to me was, "I will greatly miss your sense of humor." Nowhere in the report had he even alluded to a sense of humor, but rather painted me as a person beyond repair, who "might soon find herself in the mental health system, whether voluntarily or involuntarily." (direct quote). I am a grieving mother who just lost her only child, not a woman on the brink of insanity. Or if I am, the insanity comes from the grief, and not from anything else.

This counsellor, and I use the term loosely, brought about circumstances that made me turn inward again. He frightened me to where I wondered how others perceived me, and now didn't want to open up and trust again.

My grief still needs to be walked through and dealt with and instead I am shoving it down. I want to appear outwardly normal so no one else can say anything bad. I understand, in my head, that I gave the counsellor the power to hurt me by trusting him and opening up how I really felt. I also understand, in my head, that not everyone has to like me, but my heart says at least, they have to be fair. This counsellor made it personal and attacked me viciously when I was too weak to fight back.

Once again, am I right, or am I just a confused grieving mother? If I didn't have countless personal emails from him, no one would ever know and it would be a matter of pure conjecture, where I feel I would lose. For if you were telling me this story, who would I believe? A newly grieving mother who just lost her only child or a counsellor with credentials and a history of counselling behind him? In all actuality he never was a grief counsellor, but rather a senior's counsellor, so how he ended up counselling me was just a chain of events. I don't think you need a certificate of qualification hanging on the desk behind you to remember how to be kind. But, then, what do I know?

I'm just a grieving mother...

Day 34

This might be short, this might be long. I don't know. I've procrastinated writing all day because what is the use? What is the purpose? I'm sick and alone in Mexico, and if I didn't already have enough to complain about, this world just adds more and more and I wonder why it is this world wants to break me so bad? Why is it that people have always drawn to my sparkly personality and yet more and more and more things happen so that this personality gets broken and beaten down?

Today I feel like a big whiner. The funny thing is I also feel justified and that I have more than enough to whine about. This book is going round and round and round with all my negativity, but really, people, my son is gone, am I still supposed to be upbeat and perky? Oh, I've tried. Throughout years of consistently being beaten down, sometimes literally, my upbeat, positive personality still prevailed and I refused to let the cruelty in this world win.

What's wrong with me? Why don't I just lie down and die? Why do I keep picking myself up when it's so obvious there's no reason to try and survive? Why do I continue letting my heart beat and look for a glimmer of hope in the minutest of circumstances? My son understood. He knew we couldn't win. He knew a long time ago this world would just continue to beat him down. And it did. And I watched. And it ripped my heart apart to see him hurt. And I tried. And I continued to tell him it might get better. And I think he believed my words, but only for a time. He knew we were doomed. And doomed we were. And doomed I shall remain.

So, why can't I accept it? Why do I still look for some fairness or justice? There's none for me, just like there was none for him.

Why keep searching for this life to make sense? Why? Why? Why?

My neighbors are all out having fun, enjoying the day, while I sit here, restless and breathless, too ill to even move. When I take the dog for her morning walk, I end up gasping for air, barely able to walk back up the stairs. She waits for the next time I'll have enough energy to take her again. She never complains, she never whines, she never begs to go out. She just sits and waits because she knows I am so weak, the effort is more than I sometimes can bear.

I miss last year. I miss Tucson, Arizona. I miss the fun I had there. I miss the friends I had there. I miss the person I was there. I miss that there is where my son was still alive and I took it for granted. I just thought he would always be alive and someday he would bury me. So, I felt comfortable to hope for a better tomorrow and to see a brighter future for him and I. I felt comfortable letting my guard down and was not afraid God or this world would get me for my happiness. I felt comfortable being like a normal person who doesn't have to pay every time they are happy. I felt comfortable dreaming. I felt comfortable hoping.

Now, I no longer do and will be very careful not to try and be happy in the future.

This is just a bad, bad day. And I continue to feel like the only person not invited to the party...

Day 35

I'm tired of writing how sick I feel. I'm also tired of being as sick as I feel. Last night I wandered down the Avenida, trusty perro in hand, and could feel I was going to topple over. With the last reserve of strength left in my tenacious personality, I continued on, determined to act and feel like a real person. My wobbly legs propelled me forward to buy my eggs, bananas and milk, and when a little girl enquired as to Kelly's name, I stopped, smiled, and let her pet my perro, all the while feeling as though I could crash to the ground at any second.

I'm sick here in Mexico. I believe I've been sick for a very long time, but it seemed like my proverbial house was always burning down with other important issues so I pushed my sickness aside and persisted on. Now, it would appear my body is too unwell and a monotonous day spent lying in bed, tossing in bed, and watching TV, gives me nothing but time to think and in every circumstance, my life is found wanting and so am I.

That is why I'm tired of writing how sick I am. My existence appears to have become a continuous circle of tears, extreme sadness, extreme self-blame, extreme missing of my child, and I struggle to escape.

I used to say, "God, instead of suffering, why can't we be bowling?" and that was my determination in life. No matter what came my way, I was unwavering and fought very hard to find the moment of fun, the moment of joy, the moment of hope, the moment of love. Failure upon failure left me undaunted and purposeful to try all the harder. Friends would say I was the strongest person they knew and they marveled at how I refused to let life kick me to the curb.

"I will win", I would say, and believed it somewhere deep inside my soul. Except that "I" was a "we", but first "I" had to become whole. I had to shake off the years of abuse and trauma at the hands of my family. I had to shake off this feeling of worthlessness and sense I deserved so little in this world. I never succeeded, and to this day, struggle when people are kind, for I feel so undeserving.

When I was a little girl I remember the two most popular girls in the area befriending me. I was so thankful they would notice such an unworthy person, I dragged out all my dolls and other toys so they could play. They tired quickly and moved on, leaving me wondering what more I could have done. For I never thought I deserved love just for love's sake. I always felt I had to do something to prove myself worthy of it, and the harder I tried to be perfect, the more I failed. For no one wants a Stepford wife who smiles at the right moment, keeps you amused, never has a contradictory opinion, and basically lays herself at your feet to do with what you will.

I still struggle to show how very sad I am and will pretend, in my emails, to put on a happy face. No one from there can see me here; no one knows how sad and ill I really am. All they have is my emails and I can say and do whatever I please. Except some people care enough about me to call me on my facade and that terrifies me to no end. For I am afraid I will care too much about them, and then they, too, will be taken from me, for everything and everyone I've ever loved has been taken from me, in one form or another.

And while I know this shouldn't be all about me, and should be more about my son, I don't know all that he was feeling, but know his anguish must have been multiplied a million times more than mine, for I am here, and he is gone, and couldn't face the pain of this world anymore. Someone tried to comfort me and say at least he isn't suffering anymore, but that brings me no comfort, that brings me no relief from the pain. No one should have suffered or should still be suffering the amount of pain that would make them want to take their own life. No one should suffer so they see no other way out.

And the counsellor who I wrote about yesterday, the one who wrote such a cruel report, said to me that his son died of natural causes, but I must feel so terrible because of the stigma attached to how my son died. I hadn't felt that terrible until he brought it up, but now must admit I was one of those that would look down on a family where someone took their own life. God forgive me, and world forgive me for it was my ignorance that kept me so close minded and judgmental. I thought the family must have been a little lower class than the rest of the world for that to happen to them. I thought the person who took their life was weak in not staying behind and fighting for all they were worth. I didn't understand that suicide can hit anyone, no matter what class of people we are. I also didn't understand that someone could be brought so low and have struggled so hard and were so tired of plodding one foot in front of the other, that they couldn't see any other way out.

I also didn't want to understand the world of suicide, for it was like putting your hand in a nest of rattlesnakes. You knew you were going to end up with negative results, and in dwelling on the concept of suicide, you knew whatever you came up with was going to bring you down.

In the bible, Philippians 4:8 states: "Finally brothers, whatever things are true, whatever things are honorable, whatever things are just, whatever things are pure, whatever things are lovely, whatever things are of good report;

if there is any virtue, and if there is any praise, think about these things."

Nowhere in that scripture does it say anything about dwelling on negative, or god forbid, thinking about suicide, and we, as a society, are pressured to put forth the positive, keep a happy attitude, not bring others down by our woes, and basically, live a good life that hopefully inconveniences nobody else.

So when my friend, Brad, called me on my happy, happy attitude, I wrote back that I agreed with him and proceeded to tell him how low I really felt. All night I struggled with wondering if he would even want to be my friend after hearing all that, for I've never felt confident or comfortable enough with people to think they would still be there when the bad times came. Life and family had taught me that. I probably taught myself a little bit of that, too, for when there were people who might have held me up while I faltered and fell, I wouldn't let them. It was easier to just not have any expectations, for then you couldn't be let down.

When Brad responded the next day with a kind, warm, loving email and thanked me for sharing how I truly felt, I started to cry. He let me know it was ok not to always be upbeat and he could handle my pain. I care for him deeply, and am coming to understand, he also cares for me.

Coming back from my sojourn down the Avenida, my prizes of bananas, milk and eggs in hand, I was gasping for air and felt unable to climb the stairs. My body was perspiring profusely and felt clammy and cold. I struggled to breathe and tried to hold myself together while the room swam in front of me.

I truly am sick, lonely and alone in Mexico...

Day 36

I miss my son. I miss him terribly. I can't find words to say how I feel. I thought, in writing this daily journal, I'd be able to express the anguish inside. But the words fail me, the feelings refuse to surface and I feel stuck in this limbo between the living and the dead.

I no longer believe I belong in either world. I am no longer a functioning part of this world I live in, nor do I really care to be, and I'm not in the world of the dead, except for my heart. My heart is no longer with me, it's no longer in me, it's floating out there somewhere searching for my son. For even though I failed so horridly at being a mother, he was what filled my heart.

Please, God, I want him back. I want another chance. Please, God, I don't know all the things I did wrong, but I search my mind, I search my soul, and all the places I failed my son, I will be sure and do better next time.

Please, God, give me a next time. Please, God, don't let me live the rest of my life without him. Please, God, this is too difficult to bear. Please, God, I'm on my knees. Please, God, I'm begging you. If we're to believe your word, you raised Lazarus from the dead as his heartbroken sister looked on. You raised Jesus from the dead after He lay in a cold tomb for three days. Why can't you keep doing that? Are you not the same God the bible says you are? Is it all a bunch of mumbo jumbo meant to give false comfort and deception? Somehow I can't believe that, and while many say religious beliefs are just a crutch for broken people, I believe we all are broken in some way.

So, please, God. I can't bear to be without my son. Please, God, I can't find the words to express the anguish inside. Please, God, look into my tortured soul and see the mothers heart that can't bear this pain. Please, God, don't just pat me on the head, give me a sweet bible verse, friends to comfort, or tears to shed. Please, God, that's all fluff and stuff and of little meaning in this horrendous walk.

In the bible, Luke 11:11 states: "Which of you fathers, if your son asks for bread, will give him a stone?" So, I'm asking for a lot more than bread, why are you giving me less than a stone?

When my son first died, I had planned to have the service at a funeral home, but had asked a pastor I barely knew to say a few words. Upon arriving at the funeral home, I instantly knew the service would not be held there. Upon entering the church to greet the pastor, I also instantly knew this is where the service would be.

As the pastor did not know me well and knew my son not at all, the two of us went to the front pew and had a short talk. I told the pastor we had a hard, hard life and had overcome so much. I also told him I credited God with the fact we had overcome and stubbornly clung on to God my entire adult life. I told the pastor we had suffered a lot and God was who had brought me through. I also thought He had brought my son through, but was now proven wrong.

I told this pastor the stubbornness within me that would cling on to God and hold on for dear life was the same stubbornness that would now push Him away and never turn back again. So I asked this man of God, who had given his life's work to walk with God, to reach deep within himself and his Christianity and to somehow hear from this God I no longer trusted and say something that would make me change my mind. I was reaching out, one last time, to God and hoped He could use this man to bring me some comfort or some semblance of understanding that God was still in the house, and still able to touch my wounded spirit.

This pastor looked at me helplessly, patronizingly rubbed my back and said "God loves you", and proceeded on his way. I sat there realizing Christianity or belief in God is only for those people that already have nothing wrong in their lives. It's not for those of us that desperately need someone to hold onto and are lost and struggling to find our way.

I want so desperately to not believe that anymore, but how can I stop, when who I prayed for these 33 years, is gone?

For if it's not God's fault, then it's mine.

And my shoulders can't bear that heavy load...

Day 37

Day 37 is proving to be not much different from Day 36. No energy, no ooomph to exist, no desire to try harder to get better. I asked God today to take me, just like I've asked Him so many times before. But I had conditions to my prayer and asked it be quick and not this slow, drawn out process it apparently has become.

I see no reason left to stay. Everything I attempted in life failed. Marriage, family, love, motherhood, financial stability; everything failed. Did I somehow think myself unworthy to have any happiness so allowed things to fail? Or was I just worn out from struggling so hard in life that I ceased to try? Maybe a bit of both.

Now that my son is gone, I see no value to anything in life. I see no reason to continue to try. My friend said my life has to balance out somehow and soon there will be only good things for I definitely experienced the bad. Wanting to believe him, I inwardly know I don't. For what can replace my child? What good can possibly come to me that would make it alright that he's gone? There's nothing.

So I spiral downwards once again, while somehow wanting to find a reason to climb. There is such fruitlessness, such hopelessness, such lack of inspiration in my life now. People say time will heal and it will become easier to bear the grief but I don't really want it easier to bear. For if my child was sad enough to take his own life, what right do I, as his mother, have to be happy ever again?

And yet I know this world possesses so much happiness that is there for us to just reach out and grab. Sometimes, though, life drags us down to the point where we would have to reach up just to touch bottom and we lose the desire or ability to try.

I watched a movie the other day about a man who was told he had a year to live. He went to a grief seminar and there met a woman who worked at the university, and they fell in love. As only movies can do, it appeared she also was dying and it now was a pointless race to see who would outlive the other. He was the epitome of all she'd ever wanted in a man, and he loved her equally as well.

Being a pragmatic man, he made all sorts of rules as to how they would handle their final days with the minimum of discomfort to each other. He decided if he were to go into hospital first, she was to say goodbye at home and not come to see him. His theory was it was wisest for both of them, and she concurred.

She talked of all she would miss in life, and felt cheated, now she had met the man of her dreams, that she would never have children. Later that day, while shopping, they came across a woman who was screaming and belittling her little boy. The angry mother continued to berate until the child was in tears, and finally the couple could stand no more. The dying woman started screaming how unfair it was this woman should have children and the more she ranted, the more her indignation escalated. She took the woman's stroller, for there was also a baby in the car, and started pounding the stroller until it broke. Her anger was palpable and I felt something rise inside and then wither and die.

As happens with the best laid plans, the woman was the first to go in hospital and left a note for the man saying not to come see her. He obeyed but a millisecond and realized the foolishness of his plan, for he wanted to spend every moment allowed them with the woman he loved.

Upon seeing her weak and helpless, he put on his best face and the viewers realized he was so busy looking after things and making plans that you never saw him angry. Now it was too much to bear, so he took a sledgehammer to his newly restored custom built antique car and smashed it to smithereens. Once his car was demolished, he proceeded to smash in the ill-fated cars beside.

Once his pent up anger was released, he was able to be the support she needed and accept the unfair situation as it was.

I scream in my sleep and the words are always "No, no, no, no, no, please no." When I heard the news my son was gone, I screamed those words into the phone, but to no avail. Now I wake up with those words on my lips and wish I could feel the anger more. Getting sick has left me frustrated and slightly angry at my situation, but this anger has already been replaced with a resignation I deserve this paltry, miserable existence, and that I should not ever try anymore. It brings me a sad, false comfort that there is no longer a reason to even try. Except my day still has twenty-four hours in it that need to be filled, and these twenty-four hours are long and arduous while I just sit and wait to die. I don't know how to fill these hours and don't even know a reason to try. But when insult is added to injury and I've now paid the final price, why would more happen to me? Is there no balance to this life I live, and are some just born under lucky stars, and some meant to exist until they die? I've searched my entire life for answers and come up with none.

And that became the final message of the movie where the dying woman said to her man, "There are no answers to the questions you're asking, and we just have to accept that." He had a difficult time accepting.

As do I...

Day 38

You never know how you might touch someone's life or how someone might touch yours. It was a restless night where I dreamt my son came to visit and we were going to spend the day together. Something about him was he never demanded; he never pushed his way into a conversation or a circumstance, and he seemed to have a "whatever" attitude, giving the appearance he was fine with the outcome of anything that came his way.

Except he wasn't fine, was he? He was holding it all in and bottling it all up to where he no longer knew where to turn or how to let it out.

It saddens me he didn't feel he could come home to live. I watch other people's children come home, feeling a failure, but content that mommy and daddy will look after them until they find their way again. They might complain and be angry at their lot in life, but still feel the comfort and ease to come home.

My son wouldn't have known where home was, and when I told him I was thinking of buying in Arizona, he wouldn't have known I still had to come back to Canada for six months, and the home we have there would still be there. He wouldn't have thought to ask more questions, and instead, would have shrugged his shoulders and thought it was a closed door. He wouldn't have wanted to make me feel bad knowing how bad he felt so he would have held it all in.

Contrary to my older brother saying what a terrible child he was, my son never threw a tantrum or raised a fuss. He lived in such circumstances that it would have been pointless to demand and he rarely got his way.

It breaks my heart that his life was not one where he was surrounded by love, and family, and a confidence that he could fail, and still be loved. I will never completely know his circumstances but do know he was tired. He was tired of the fight, just as I'm tired of it now. He was the reason I continued to fight in this world, he was the reason I continued to believe and hope, he was the reason I took step after step, and like I've said so many times before, I no longer have a reason.

Yet, I failed. I failed to instill in my son the belief that he had as much right to be in this world as anyone else. I failed to instill in him the belief there could be a better way.

For I didn't know the better way myself and not only did I fail him, I failed myself.

These were the thoughts in my mind when I woke up from the dream where my son was still present, very much alive, and visiting me here on earth.

My mind was troubled, hopeless and helpless in a fight I could no longer win. For no matter what comes my way in this lifetime, the battle for my son's safety and healing was lost. It was the most important battle I'd ever waged, and losing it became my undoing.

Upon opening my front door to take Kelly for her morning walk, I saw a plastic bag hanging on my door. Inside the bag was a package of chicken noodle soup, left by my neighbor Jan. I barely knew this woman and yet she had reached out in kindness, knowing I was ill. To her it was a package of soup; to me it was a straw to grasp onto in this disturbing day.

We never know what act or deed or kindness may touch another human being, and we never know that what we've done may have been the only thing to touch them their entire day.

I am learning a lot in this walk; I just hate the reason why.

Today I go to the doctor to see what my test results are. No one was able to give me a ride and I am contemplating walking the long way. Why am I doing this? Is it to save the cost of a taxi? Maybe. It doesn't make sense because the taxi ride is twenty pesos and the doctor's visit is five hundred pesos. Sometimes I don't understand my rationale, but walk it, I may.

Day 39

Walking to the doctor's office I felt tired and faint, but mildly invigorated at finally being able to do something. I was still gasping for air, and the doctor was perplexed that this latest round of heavy antibiotics still had not done the trick. I told him my liver/pancreas area was very sore and causing me a lot of pain, almost to the point of burning. He took this to mean I had acid reflux and proceeded to give me pills. When I told him I didn't have acid reflux and it was more of a stabbing pain to the liver area, he then gave me strong pain medications and more antibiotics.

I felt the frustration so often felt in Canada where I just was not being heard. The same complaint never deviated as it came from my lips, and yet so many different doctors heard it in so many different ways, and here I was, seven years later, sicker and weaker than before.

When I feel this deep frustration, instead of fighting for my rights or making myself heard, some inner bell goes off that tells me it's pointless and fruitless to try, so I give up. This giving up attitude I seem to embrace then fills me with self-blame for not trying harder.

Now trying to muster up any hope for a future is an insurmountable task, so when my doctor doesn't understand what I'm trying to say, I simply resign myself to the futility of trying to get well.

We were the paradox, my son and I. While life repeatedly knocked us down, we continued to rise, until finally, he had no strength to rise any more.

Just one more time, son, just one more time...

Sufficiently saturated with prescription drugs, I deduced last night would be a good night to cut down on my sleeping medications. The doctor thought my new habit of sleeping ten to twelve hour days was a sign of understandable depression. While I agreed some of it was depression, I also thought it was the sleep aids and total lethargy brought about by my illness.

Cutting back on one sleep aid saw me rudely awake at 4 a.m. and there I stayed. My friend, Heidi, was coming to get me the next morning at 10:00 a.m., so the sleeplessness was further intensified knowing I couldn't sleep in. Many hours of tossing and turning finally produced a dream filled sleep where I was looking at pictures of my son. It was the first time since his passing I allowed myself to look on his face and I could feel my moaning in my sleep. The pain of missing him brings tears to my eyes as I sit writing this journal. I ache to see him again, I ache to hug him again, I ache to give bad advice and hear him resignedly say, "no worries" or "take care" or "I love you, mom."

I ache inside. Please, God, either take away the ache or me...

Day 40

I may soon leave Mexico. My friend, Brad, who lives in Oregon, but also has a home in Tucson, Arizona, has been inviting me to come for Christmas, and now he says I can just rent his house in Arizona and stay the spring, after he's gone back home.

Like most decisions in my life, I'm vacillating. Do I stay or do I go? I have always let fear guide and manipulate my life and many times let the decisions make themselves. Eventually whatever dilemma of the day I may be facing comes to a critical point and many times I take the path of least resistance, hoping for a positive outcome.

The more I write this journal, the more I don't like myself, but think a lot of the dislike comes from the defeat I feel at the outcome of mine and my son's life. If he were alive today, all my foibles and follies and lack of direction in life would be just fodder for discussion with my friends as they too, would lament decisions that brought them disastrous results.

As it stands I now thrash myself for every life choice, no matter how small, for the outcome my son and I received is its own recompense.

Part of me thinks I haven't totally given Mexico a chance and am just further running away. The other part of me wonders if I'm just looking to recreate the happy times I had last winter in Arizona and I may be sorely disappointed. I know, with Brad, I feel safe and secure, but once he leaves I will be left to my own devices, and the people who knew me last year would not recognize the person I've become.

I also wonder if this is the time for Brad and me to see if we might have a relationship in the making. It seems ludicrous to even consider a relationship at this time in my life, and maybe I'm gravitating towards a place of comfort and kindness and want it to be more. This is a lonely journey and he sometimes makes it bearable and supports me, without fail, during this great sadness. I am afraid to fall in love with him, because if it didn't work out, and I lost him, I don't think I could take more loss.

And yet, all the times I've been afraid to take a chance has brought me to where I am now; alone and lonely in Mexico.

Yesterday my friends, Pete and Heidi, came to town and I went for lunch. Sitting there brought about a dizziness I've rarely experienced and with it came the downpour of sweat. I know I'm unwell, and am equally frustrated I am so limited in anything I do.

After Pete left, Heidi and I sat at the restaurant and did what we always do; we talked about our sons. After more than four years, her tears are quick to the surface and she talks as though her loss happened yesterday. She tries to reassure me that time will squelch the pain somewhat, but I still see so much pain in her. While this isn't a contest where there is a winner and a loser, as we've both lost, I still say Heidi has a husband of many years, a loving daughter and son-in-law, a grandchild and other than living her life without her son, is living a full life. That is not to say her pain isn't as deep as mine, it just appears she has so much more to live for than I, for I have none of the things she has. I know I tried hard to attain them and sometimes laid down my own desires and will in hopes of achieving my goal, but it all came to no fruition and my dreams of a peaceful, loving life were never attained.

If my son were still alive, it wouldn't matter so much.

I woke myself up screaming last night...

I wonder if I am in the right place where the grief is able to rise up, or am I punishing myself further by being so alone?

Day 41

Today I feel sad. I feel sad because I'm so sick and am quite sure I have pancreatitis, for all the symptoms are prevalent. It's not my first time at this tea party and seven years ago, during a routine scope down my throat, the surgeon zigged when he should have zagged and cut my pancreas quite severely. While I was treated for seven days in the hospital where I drifted in and out of consciousness, one day, when my hospital bed was needed by another patient, I was declared miraculously cured and released, still barely able to walk.

What proceeded was seven years of agony with vain attempts to convince a massive amount of doctors that I was still ill, only to be met with either blank looks of bewilderment or resistance to help me, followed by a patronizing pat on the head and useless advice to go for a long walk and enjoy the sunshine.

Finally, like so many things in my life, I just stopped talking and trying to find a cure for my malaise. Thus began a succession of what I seem to do best; ignoring the symptoms, living on pain medications and accepting this was to be my lot in life. Only I knew I was functioning at twenty percent of the person I used to be, and only I knew I wasn't looking for symptoms which didn't exist.

Now, the abdominal pain is so excruciating, nothing alleviates. This doctor looks as flummoxed as the rest and the dizziness is so extreme, I have no concentration or ability to explain myself further. The only thing I do know is my symptoms are all of pancreatitis, and while I've asked God many times to take me, could I not be granted the privilege of it being quick?

I'm sad because I may soon have to tell Brad I won't be coming to Arizona. In our daily emails we're making plans as to what we will do and see while I'm there and I've come to realize that it doesn't matter anymore if I go to Arizona; what I really want is to spend time with Brad.

I now correspond with the two ladies I'd met from Nova Scotia, Canada, and one of them lost her husband this year. We talk about the grief and while the circumstances to our loss are different, some of our coping mechanisms are the same. Yesterday she sent me an email saying she avoids anything negative and credits that to her being unable to also make big decisions. I hadn't fully understood I was doing that. Your mind, soul, body, very essence of who you are, is so immersed in the grief, you have not even an iota of strength left for anything else. Her email made me realize I want everything to just exist around me and have no more surprises, no more losses, no more negatives of any kind.

While I know Brad will be understanding and kind if I tell him I'm not coming, it still is a negative outcome to what could be a very positive experience. He has put out the olive branch in trying to help any way he can and it is now up to me to reach back and grab on. My fear causes hesitation, all the while knowing my heart is already open and vulnerable to this man.

Friends say to just trust that everything will work out as it should, but I've bought into that concept before, only to be met with disastrous results. For, if I'm to believe life will unfold as it ought to, then that would mean my son was meant to die when he was only thirty-three years old. That would mean I was meant to be left, drifting in this bewilderment at how this all came about.

That would mean there is someone in control who could have our lives be rich and full and loving. That would mean someone cared about my son and I. I no longer believe that and feel my life was of no purpose; it had no reason or rhyme.

I want my life to mean something.

I want my son's life to have had a purpose...

Day 42

Poznekoff, Pity Party table for one, your table is ready. My imagination takes flight and I see a concierge bellowing those words as I sit here, wishing for something good to happen. I have an opportunity to be in Arizona and it does not look as though it will work out. I am finding I miss Brad more than I miss Arizona and think it's really him I want to be with. He is comfort and a place of safety for me, in a world I no longer feel comfortable or safe in.

Truthfully though, something deep inside tells me I'm where I'm supposed to be and need to deal with grief, instead of running away yet again. I ran to Mexico because home was unbearable, now I'm in Mexico and want to run to Arizona. In all fairness to me, for sometimes I do tire of beating myself up, I have legitimate reasons to feel sad, to feel down and depressed, and why should I be faulted for searching somewhere that would bring me but a moments respite from the turmoil churning within?

My son and I always thought we had to take the path less travelled by others and endure whatever came our way. Others would run from affliction while we thought it made us strong to overcome. It didn't make us strong. It made us tired and worn out. People told me my entire adult life that I was strong. I saw that statement as an insult rather than a compliment for I just struggled to survive. I would rather be someone who doesn't know what losing her son feels like. I would rather be someone who didn't survive the loss of her son. I would rather be someone who was asleep, not to awaken, because then this pain would not be present in me. And I wouldn't have to be strong.

Last night I writhed in pain and only slept under the influence of sleep medications. I awoke early as I needed to be at the lab by 8 a.m.

Numerous tests resulted in a bill of $200 U.S. and I saw how ludicrous my rationale was when it came to finances. I watched every penny and was careful of purchases, always opting to buy the cheaper or not at all, and here I was, after a few weeks, almost a thousand dollars poorer due to my lack of health. My counters are lined with medications and prescriptions all written in Spanish so I am at the mercy of a doctor, trusting he is prescribing pills that will make me well.

The lab told me my results would be to the doctor by Friday and so I wait again. By the time I walked back to my apartment and my waiting perro, the wind was out of me and my lungs were gasping for air. I wonder how much of this is brought on by stress due to the passing of my son, and how much of it is from previous ailments. I feel more distressed than I thought possible and that any happiness is always just inches from my reach. For, here I sit, alone, lonely and sick in Mexico and yet, there is merriment, enjoyment, caring and concern awaiting me in Arizona.

Or is that just my hope?

Day 43

Today brings more whining, more complaining, more drama, and more continuation of the saga that is my life. Yesterday, while doing the ultrasound, the technician said all my intestines were inflamed and this would account for the excruciating pain I'm in. Since getting that information, I have researched inflamed intestines and come up with a myriad of diseases; the most prevalent one being pancreatitis, which encompasses all of my symptoms, while the other diseases only circumvent the principle ones.

Before I could begin the second paragraph of this day's musings and events, my friend, Heidi, came by. Tomorrow is my son's birthday and I am sorely grieving the fact he is not here for me to call on his special day. December 15, 1976 was the best day of my life. It was the day I finally felt complete as a human being and looked wondrously on this tiny baby that came out of my body, given to me to love.

How can it be that he's no longer here and I feel this empty hole in my heart that should be filled with excitement on this event, what would have been his 34th birthday? Now, he will forever remain 33 and I will forever lament the day of his death, instead of celebrating the day of his birth.

I really can't write more about it for I feel the panic and sorrow want to rise to the top and I'm pushing it down with all that is within me.

Heidi and I were to spend the day together tomorrow in Puerto Vallarta as I didn't want to be alone, but when she saw me this morning, she saw what I already knew, that I would not be well enough to spend an entire day busy in a big city. We've still agreed to meet in the morning and will wait and see what the day brings, for now so much rests on how I feel.

I think I am better today or maybe it's that the restlessness and boredom have reached gargantuan proportions and will no longer be subdued. Whatever the reason, once Heidi left, I donned my running shoes and Kelly and I ventured out to walk the distance to Rincon de Guayabitos, the next town over. I sometimes question the wisdom of my decisions, but many times want to run and hide from the constant sadness and negativity that is my life, so want to tire myself out so much that I can't think or feel. I rarely succeed.

Kelly was a willing participant in my escapade of today and upon arriving at the beach in Guayabitos, we proceeded to play our favorite game of throw the stick into the ocean for the perro. The perro seems tireless in her quest for the elusive stick and will continue playing throughout the day.

Since seeing the two snakes my first week in Mexico, I had been hesitant to enter the water, but today threw caution to the wind and allowed myself to wade in. As the warm waves lapped against my legs, I felt a moment of joy and a sense of peace, and wanted the moment to continue and the feeling to stay.

While jumping over the waves, I convinced myself the snake sightings were a rare circumstance and determined to wear my bathing suit next time and swim further out. Exiting the water and walking a short distance with Kelly, there it was, sunning itself by the ocean shore; a snake, writhing and twisting in all its ugliness.

I give up.

Kelly and I played stick for over an hour and then continued on our way to the opposite end of the town. People commented on what a well behaved dog I had and how she walked beside me without a leash and never deviated from staying close to my side. The sadness hit me and I wanted to tell the people that my son would have had it no other way. He would have made sure he left a well-trained and loving dog to watch over me. He would have made sure I was as well looked after as he could leave me.

Once again, I can't continue to talk about my son as I feel as though I will implode. This is too painful and today I can think of nothing or no one else than my son.

Kelly the dog and I reached the end of the beach and sat to soothe our tired feet. Watching the ocean waves, I thought about my son and felt the sorrow sweep over me to where I saw no release. It seemed like seconds I sat there, but know it was much longer. Finally, Kelly nudged my hand and let me know it was time to go.

We trudged back the way we came and arrived home exhausted, winded and cold. I may have overdone, which is what I do. Even though it is only early evening I want to crawl into bed and there I will stay. I'm tired, cold, in a lot of pain, and want to see my son. I miss him and wish so many things were so different than what they were. Mostly I wish the outcome was different and he was the one to bury me. I would have taken his place and wish I had the choice.

He did call me before he did this awful deed and told me it was very important I call him back. If I had only tried harder, he may still be alive today. What was wrong with me? Why didn't I fight harder to help my child? Now, friends tell me to fight hard to survive, but it seems ludicrous. My son didn't have a chance. Why should I?

Tonight I will eventually sleep and then tomorrow will be another day. It won't just be any day; it will be one of sadness instead of joy. It will be a day of sorrow instead of celebration. It will be another day without my son.

Day 44

Today is my son's birthday.
There is nothing left to say...

Day 45

Just because today is no longer his birthday doesn't mean I feel any better. Yesterday was a day spent hoping this experience would become liminal, and I know I've endeavored greatly to push the grief away.

Not having cried for a few days, I somehow convinced myself I was growing stronger, or accepting the fact my son was dead, or just at a place of resignation where I deserved no happiness in life and all I would put my hope upon would fail. Some resistance inside told me there still was a chance for some joy, if only I could push past or immerse myself and subsequently walk through this enormous tidal wave of sorrow that encompassed my soul.

I don't know what I'm doing. I don't know the proper way to grieve my son. I don't know how to stop the enormous amount of guilt I feel. Obviously everything I've ever done in my life was wrong for this was the outcome. My son is gone. How can anything ever feel right again?

Heidi and I went to Walmart, about an hour's drive from here. I bought her lunch but mine was tasteless to me. I conversed politely but remember nothing that was said. I wandered the aisles of Walmart but my shopping cart remained empty.

Many times I would feel the tears start to rise and as before, would push them away. Feeling dead inside and remorseful for all I had said or not said to my son, every scenario played itself over and over in my mind. None brought any relief and I faulted every slight done to him as the ultimate push for him to do what he had done.

Heidi said I needed to yell and get it out because she could sense I was holding so much in. I am holding it in, but told her I can't just force it to come out. She yelled loudly in the truck, hoping to inspire me to do the same, but all it did was make me feel shy and nervous to let my voice be heard. People seem so free to just be who they are and know they will still be accepted and loved. I don't remember ever having that freedom, or ever allowing my son to.

No matter where I look, what I think, what others say, I am to blame. I am to blame for his death. I am to blame that he's gone. I am to blame.

Coming home in the truck, my tears finally came. They would not be held back any longer. Once the dam burst and the floodgates opened, I wanted my friend to understand everything that happened in our lives. I jumped from subject to subject, sometimes talking about my own neglect and failings as a mother; sometimes talking about my family and what they had done to us and how hard it was for me to be mother, father, brother, sister, grandma, grandpa, cousin, uncle, auntie, friend. It was all so hard and I went over scenario after scenario, explaining to my friend how afraid I was, wanting her to say something, anything to release me from my guilt. I wanted someone to understand that I had a mother's heart, but couldn't do it on my own. I desperately needed help and support and when I turned for that help and support, I was turned away. I was told to handle my own problems and no one wanted to get involved. I was told I must deserve the painful life I was leading or God would intervene. I was told so many wrong things, but the end result was I finally stopped asking for anyone to help us and just did the best I could on my own. And my son suffered. And I suffered.

But, I am still alive.

Day 46

I procrastinated all morning sitting down to write. I keep saying to friends that I don't know what to say, all the while saying I am missing my son so terribly and feeling so much pain. I repeat the same words over and over again and can't find the words to fully portray the anguish within.

This is too hard to bear. It is just too hard. I can't stop crying and it makes me feel no better. I don't know what to say. I wish it was me instead of him. That is the right way. Not this. Never this. Why does it have to be this way?

I don't know how to go on without him and I should have been able to call him and wish him a happy birthday. He would have joked around, made me laugh, and I would have marveled at having such a wonderful son. I miss him so much.

He was my heart and now he's gone and I can't take the pain. I can't find a place of peace anywhere. This will never be ok and I will never be ok and I hate that I have to stay behind. I don't know how to fill the hours of the day and I no longer even want to try.

When he died, I died. No parent should ever have to know how this feels. I just don't know what else to say.

Other than I'm still very sick here in Mexico and today I go for my results. That is another thing I'm procrastinating doing as it is just more negative upon the negative that already exists. My entire life has been a struggle to find some hope and some joy. Getting knocked down and knocked down has kept me watchful and afraid, but still determined to try. Even now, I still try, for the alternative is too difficult to bear. I can't live in this sadness all the time because then I don't want to live at all.

And I know why I held off writing today. Because I either would write how I'm truly feeling and then the tears would flow, or I would write about frivolous, nonsensical subjects, just hoping to fill the page. Writing about mundane things leaves me more frustrated than ever, and yet sometimes I don't want to write about the pain inside. I want it to just sit there and leave me alone, just for a second, a moment, or a day. I want everything to go right and nothing to go wrong. I want the sun to shine and for it to never rain. I want my friends to write me only loving, caring emails and never tell me what to do. I want to hear from Brad every day for I cling onto his words. I am afraid at how attached I am to him, for I've lost everything I've ever cared about, and now am afraid I will lose him too.

So I'm racing against time, trying to get well, trying to get happier, just so my decision whether or not to go to Tucson will be a logical one. All the while, I know I'm not going, and wonder if this is just another opportunity lost. I'm going to sit here sad, sick, and alone in Mexico while there could be so much more.

And I see how in life, many times I've chosen the path that will bring me less joy, for if I was truly happy and more sadness came, then it's too far to fall. Better not to climb too high for then the crash to the bottom is not so far. I learnt this well while still very young and when I would gingerly, warily cross my toe into the threshold of a better life, it would get viciously stomped on and I would retreat, careful to not try again for a very long time. But try again I would, for inside me is a woman who refused to give up. I refused to totally fail at this thing called life, and so continued to try, only to fail again.

This was the ultimate failure and the ultimate pain and the ultimate kick to my tenaciousness and determination for a better life.

It was the final blow.

Why do I continue to try and rise?

Day 47

I had two choices today; to wallow in self-pity and tell all about it in this daily journal, or simply not to write. Most of the day I chose not to write, but then I'm drawn, like a moth to a flame, and find myself sitting at my computer telling about my day.

I woke up way too early because of the extreme physical pain in my stomach and right side. The pain made me irritable and feeling as though I simply cannot win. Yesterday my doctor asked me if I believed in God, and today I want to say, yes, I believe in Him. I believe I am his punching bag and cruel joke to the world where he laughs at how much misery and pain a human can endure. Some may say, "Don't talk like that, Nina, that's not God you're describing", but before you judge me, you would need to know more about my life.

You would need to know it was a life full of joyless misery where at every turn, I was pushed down. Every time I tried to rise up, I was kicked to the ground. And still I believed. Still I thought there was a loving God who was watching and would soon reward, or at least ease the suffering somewhat. He didn't and my son was to die, showing me in no uncertain terms, that in this life, we were doomed.

It's as if we are cursed and God is not strong enough to break the curse or to have let us live even a mediocre life.

So with grieving the loss of my only child here in Mexico, I also have to deal with physical ailments that cause me so much pain. I am dizzy, lightheaded, losing my balance, and unable to finish a sentence without gasping. I can't even have a simple conversation without the room swimming in front of me and feel as though I will pass out from the simple exertion of taking my dog out for a pee.

I'm frustrated beyond belief. I'm frustrated and if you were telling me this story, I would have a hard time believing, because surely no one human being could endure all this.

Well, apparently they can, for I am.

But I'm not enduring happily. I'm gloomy and miserable and regret the day I was born. I'm sick and I'm tired and I'm lonely and it hurts to even breathe. I wish I was dead, I truly do.

For what purpose is there to want to live anymore?

None.

Day 48

I keep threatening to not write every day. I want to quit writing altogether, so then why do I go on? I think my life has to mean something and I wonder if someday someone will be reading my words and, having gone through the death of a child, will find some comfort in what I say.

It's a frightening journey, this one where you lose your child. You don't act like you used to act, you don't think like you used to think, and you wonder if your life could ever have a purpose now.

I know, with continually feeling sick, I'm losing any energy I used to have to write, and even if my child were alive, the level of sickness I feel makes me grimace at the thought of having to do anything at all. Every sad event continues to be compounded in my life and I see no break, no relief, no respite, no moment of pleasure.

The doctor wants to put me on many antidepressants because he feels the sadness is the major problem. I've listened to doctors before and ended up only being a lab rat, used for experimentation, and sicker than I began. Now I want to be heard and want the doctor to understand he needs to deal with the cause for the pain. Then it will at least give me a brief moment where I can continue to deal with the grief. Why is so much negative always happening? Why can't I be here, grieving my son, but at least be allowed the privilege of good health? I don't understand.

Today I wrote Brad and told him it was pretty definite I wouldn't be coming to Tucson. Just another happy time that, naturally, I'm not allowed to have. When people tell me to grab on to any joyful occasion that comes my way, I want them to explain to me how that could be brought about? How can I grab on to anything joyful when it would appear I'm to be brought down wherever I turn.

I was so upset by having to tell him I'm not coming that I couldn't sit in this apartment today. Kelly the dog and I went walking to Rincon de Guayabitos and I spent part of the day throwing the stick in the ocean to Kelly and walking the length of the beach. Children came up to play with Kelly and I let them throw the stick in the water. Their childlike laughter rang throughout the beach as Kelly jumped the ocean waves, intent on her prey. The children were so easily entertained and amused and the mothers thanked me for letting them play with my grande perro. It could have been a happy day, but there is no rest for my soul. There's no joy inside. There's only turmoil and negativity and illness and a wanting to die.

The doctor is right. I am depressed. I am also very sick and in a lot of pain. I need to feel better physically so my mind can be clearer and I can make decisions to go or to stay. The way I feel now, the thought of leaving Mexico leaves me exhausted beyond explanation, and so here I stay.

Coming back from Guayabitos I felt hungry and tired and unwell and wanted to eat and lie down. My neighbor, Jan, knocked on my door and wanted to visit for a while. Simple conversation is tiring, so we went downstairs to the games room and played a few games of pool. By the time we were finished, my head was swimming, I was nauseous and could barely wait to lie down. I just want to feel better and do something as simple as play. It's doesn't seem to be for me.

Now I sit here, pain in my stomach, wanting to pass out, confused as to what to do or say. When I try and take a deep breath, my head swims, and I feel so unwell, the simplest task escapes me.

Do you ever feel your grasp is always just one inch away from happiness? I've lived my life that way.

Why do I keep trying?

Day 49

I no longer know what to say. The pain in my liver/pancreas area woke me up at 3 a.m. and wide awake is where I stayed. Irritated, frustrated and agitated, I took some anxiety relief drugs and tried to sleep. Still sick and tired of being sick and tired, I tossed and turned fitfully, trying to find a place that felt right, which is an effort in futility and the sublime bordering on the ridiculous, for nothing has felt right since my son passed away.

The agitation continued throughout the night and was exacerbated by the constant pain. The doctor is sticking firm my principle ailment is depression, and while I do agree I am depressed, I still believe there is something medically wrong. If you question a doctor and disagree with them, they get angry and want to dismiss you, so after disagreeing with him once, I was careful not to do so again.

Everything bugged me, everyone bugged me, nothing was going right, nothing would ever go right again. I can't have what I want, which is my son still alive, so everything else not working out just adds to the sad, and adds to the mad.

After telling Brad I wasn't coming to Tucson, I've felt agitated all day. I know I would be happy doing things and going places with him, and right now, do believe I need him more than he needs me. I wonder if somehow I have replaced my reliance and communication with my child, to my reliance and communication with him, and when I sense him slipping away, feel the grief at the loss of my child more. I don't know. I'm all confused and turned around and up seems down, wrong seems right, and truly

I must be like Alice in Wonderland as she fell down the rabbit hole. Only her life was fiction; my life is real. My life will continue as long as it will, but the reality is it will be without my son.

I wish I had words to properly describe my feelings. The sense of injustice, the sense of hopelessness, the deep sense of loss, the overwhelming longing and desire to see him again; nothing even comes close to describing how I feel.

This is wrong, God.

This is so wrong.

Trudging my sleepless, pain filled body to the doctor's office, the sun beat down upon me. Already irritated at life, the fact the doctor was not in intensified my exasperation, and as I sat waiting for almost an hour, the exhaustion beat at me like a drum. I wanted sleep so badly, but it was not to be. Walking back home, I stopped in to see my friend, Babs, hoping for a brief respite from the sad, but she had her own woes and proceeded to recite her own lackluster life. It only added to my sense of doom and gloom and my steps were a little slower and my head hung down a little lower as I proceeded on my journey home.

Kelly greeted me barking her welcome and it irritated and annoyed. Poor Kelly the dog. She only wanted me to know she was happy to see me.

Later in the afternoon, upon returning to the doctor's office, he was not in the greatest of moods. He firmly told me I have colitis, which maybe I do, and shushed any protest that I didn't have the symptoms. He also informed me there was quite an outstanding bill and I quickly promised to pay the next time. As I started to cry, he advised I needed to learn to control the crying and deal with this depression. Duly noted, I was dismissed until the next time.

I feel angry, but don't know how to deal with the anger. I've lost at this game of life, and hate that I continue to get beaten down. I'm afraid for tomorrow, have no care for today, and yearn for a yesterday where my son was alive.

This has been a terrible, terrible day and I am glad it is over.

Day 50

I hate stupid doctors. I hate doctors who don't know what they are talking about. This Mexican doctor says I have colitis and depression and nothing else. He tells me to force myself to stop crying.

I just lost my son. How do I stop crying?

He also wants me on many antidepressants, but I told him if only some of the pain were to subside, the depression would not be so prominent. I asked him over and over to first get me well, and then we could work on the depression, but his mind was made up and he didn't want to hear anything I had to say.

Last night, in sheer frustration at the duration of this illness, I took some anti-inflammatory pills the doctor back home had prescribed. I also took pain medication, as well as the sleeping pills. It was the first good sleep I'd had since I got sick and this morning, the twist tie to the stomach pain had lessened somewhat. Whether my illness has just run its course, or I ingested the right cocktail of meds, I don't know, but my symptoms did improve.

While I never am happy anymore, my mood still lifted from the sour, dour, mopey, dopey person I had become this past month. The outdoors beckoned me, people interested me, my presentation mattered, and I cuddled my dog.

Walking Kelly for her morning pee, we passed a Mexican woman who had previously informed me her name was Gigi. Gigi spoke no English, my Spanish was minimal, and we co-existed with hand gestures all the while speaking our own language loudly, hoping that would make us better understood. It didn't, but somehow Gigi was always waiting on her stoop whenever Kelly and I walked by. She was a colorful woman and might have been interesting to get to know. She was always dressed in bright colors and wore sequined dresses, even throughout the day. Years of smoking had darkened her teeth, but she continued sucking on the ever present cigarette, complete with long ash just waiting to fall. She seemed excited whenever she saw Kelly and me and today beckoned us over. As I crossed the street to her modest home, she presented me with a plastic Santa Claus bowl and seemed eager to have me take it. Not wanting to offend and thanking her profusely for her kindness, my step had a bounce to it as I walked home, Christmas present in hand. It was my first present, and undoubtedly would be my last this Christmas season, but her small gesture of sharing brought me a brief moment of joy.

As today was the maid's day to clean, Kelly and I headed to the beach in Guayabitos, where we played the never tiring game of throw the stick into the ocean. Many would stop and watch as Kelly circumvented the ocean waves and proudly brought her stick to shore.

Heading back found me winded and gasping for air. The tiredness seemed to permeate my body and reaching our destination proved to be a struggle.

It still was the best day we've had so far, and while the rest of the day was spent resting, I saw my mood lift at the small reprieve from this illness. The doctor was wrong. I may be depressed, but there is still something more.

Right now I'm too tired to care.

Day 51

Last night I took many pain medications, along with some anti-anxiety pills which should have helped with the agitation. Mixed in with my sleeping pills, my night was interspersed with upsetting dreams while I slept and tears running down my face while I lay awake.

Am I going crazy? Am I losing my mind? Do I appear to be quite normal on the outside, but is my inside emotional state all mixed up? I think I'm doing things quite logically and all my actions appear normal, but when I search out an item, it's always been misplaced; when I'm looking for information that before would have been meticulously organized, nothing has been done.

I've been told when you're in grief you have no room for anything else and so appear to be quite scatterbrained. While I understand this concept in a logical, methodical way, it puts me in a panic when I can't grab ahold of the simplest concept, nor do I much care. I should care. I'm still living in this world, lost somehow between this world and the world beyond, but until I can go to be with my son, I need to function.

How?

Today was to be spent filling out the multitude of medical forms in hopes of recouping some of the money I've spent here on doctors and labs. I'm frustrated with this doctor and have no confidence he knows what he's doing. Everything is chocked up to depression and while I don't disagree depression is one of my ailments, I also believe there's more. He infuriates me because he's not hearing what I have to say, dismisses my questions, and like always, when faced with confrontation, I back away.

Money matters cause me a great deal of concern probably because my life has financially always been such a struggle. If I could have helped my son more, maybe he would still be alive.

I can't do this today. I can't just write nonsensical riffraff about my nonsensical day. I can't ask question after question for what matters the answer? What does it matter if, from now on, everything in my life is perfect, for my son is gone?

What does it matter?

I can't do this today.

I don't care to write or talk or feel or cry.

It's two days before Christmas and who cares? My son never had a good Christmas with me anyways, so what does it matter that it's Christmas Day? All my hopes and dreams for a happy family never materialized. He deserved better. He didn't deserve to die. He deserved to be surrounded by loving family and friends. He deserved to be loved, protected, and cherished much more than he was.

Who loved my son, God?

I loved my son, God! It just turned out all wrong, and I didn't show him enough how much I loved him. In the end, he felt he had nowhere to turn. He probably didn't, and I will carry that until my dying day.

Please be merciful, God, and let it be soon...

Day 52

Today was a better day, mostly because my physical health had improved. Walking with Kelly to the Thursday market had my step lighter and my countenance brighter for I was looking forward to the clatter, clamor and hubbub of the day. By the time we reached the village square, my steps dragged laboriously and the question arose as to whether I may have bitten off more than I could chew.

Undaunted and steadfast, I persevered in my search for the perfect vegetables and rich, ripe fruit. Meeting my friends, Heidi and Pete, made me happy to see people I cared about and cared about me. We went for lunch with many of their other friends, and the mood was lighthearted and cheerful.

My landlady had invited me, along with Heidi and Pete, for Christmas Eve dinner tomorrow night and they were touched to be included. It would be a time of merriment and I needed to immerse myself in a happy time, no matter how fleeting it may be.

By the time lunch was done, so was I. Returning to the apartment, feeling light headed and dizzy, my chest began to ache. The feverish sweat started to glisten on my brow and I felt defeated at the possibility I may get the bronchitis or lung infection back again. It always seems as though I'm surrounded by darkness, and when I try and break out, even a tiny bit, get knocked down and knocked down. Many would say not to entertain those thoughts, but how do I not?

Everything bad that had happened in my life until now could be forgotten and put aside, with still the search for the elusive happiness I yearned for since a child. Not anymore. Now, nothing is as it should be and nothing is worthwhile doing and nothing is worth hoping for. Not now, and probably not ever again.

This afternoon was yet another doctor appointment and I knew I had many previous visits yet to pay for. I no longer think he's a stupid doctor and regret having written that some chapters ago, but do find now my emotions run amuck as though they have a will of their own. Prior to my son's passing, I was the epitome of politeness and could hold my tongue when needed, and sometimes even when I should have spoken up, so this new person I've become who gets so easily upset and is sure everything will go wrong and everyone is out to get her, is quite the surprise, and admittedly, not a pleasant one. One saving grace is I don't speak my feelings to people who upset me, and since I no longer trust my own logic or power of reasoning, have learned to hold it all in. Since I've held in my emotions most of my life, it's not that difficult a task, but yet now sometimes surprise myself at the mundane events which inwardly cause me such grief.

Upon reaching the doctor's office, I was gasping for air. He told me I should only be walking a maximum of three blocks a day and still should rest, as I had been very ill and his concern was I would become that ill again. I told him resting was very difficult for me as the only way I've found to deal with my grief, even in the smallest of proportions, is to walk great distances at a rapid pace. This doctor then admitted losing a child of his own some twenty years ago, and as I sat waiting for him to tell me I still needed to rest and not walk, he surprised me by agreeing that the only way he dealt with his grief, even after all this time, was to immerse himself in his work. He said keeping busy is the only way to make the day go by until someday he will be reunited with his child again.

He asked me, for a second time, if I believed in God. I told him yes, but right now, had a difficult time believing God believed in me.

Heidi and Pete have also told me the only way they can endure each day is by keeping so busy working that the day passes by. What are we all running away from, we grieving parents? Are we hoping that by running fast enough, we can stay one step ahead of the grief that would lift us up and sweep us away? As I sit and try to rest, it would certainly appear so.

Then, this kind doctor told me he was going to waive the cost of some of my doctor visits and only charge me for the prescriptions he filled. That made me cry and I put out my hand to shake his and wish him a happy holiday.

Instead, he came around his desk and gave me a huge hug and told me I need to search for some happiness somewhere.

I told him I would try...

Day 53

Today is Christmas Eve. I don't want to write.

Day 54

Today is Christmas Day. I don’t want to write today either.

Day 55

I still don't want to write. I've had many other days where I didn't want to write, but I wrote anyways. Christmas Eve, Christmas Day and today, Boxing Day, I just can't seem to muster up the energy anymore.

I am in a depression.

I am in a deep, deep depression.

For me to not be able to put on a smile or even a reasonable facsimile of a happy face is unheard of.

My son is gone.

What reason would I have to smile?

With it being the Christmas season, and with people coming here for a vacation, it is a time of merriment and festivities. Each burst of laughter is like sandpaper scraping my wounded soul. Each loud guffaw causes me to cringe inside and want to run away.

So, I am running away.

Today I booked a ticket to Tucson, Arizona to see Brad and will be gone for five days.

Already I'm nervous at the dog being fine here without me; I'm nervous it will be too traumatic for me being in Tucson; I'm basically nervous at life.

As I sit and listen to my neighbors laugh uproariously, I just want them to shut up. What could there possibly be to be that happy about? Probably the fact their daughter just arrived for the Christmas vacation would give them reason for joy.

I know I have caring. I know I have support. I know I have people who care about me and want to help. They are all as helpless as I am and none of us know what it will take for me to survive this horror of all horrors.

Should I have only booked a one way ticket to Tucson and spent the rest of the winter there? Should I have packed up my dog, instead of leaving her here with friends? Should I have taken a chance that Arizona would still hold the magic it held for me last year?

Decision making is overwhelming and I somehow just want to be left alone, with no more disasters happening and someone else making the decisions. I want someone to care enough about me to cook my meals, make sure I get enough sleep, and hug me at least once a day. I don't want to be alone and have to deal with normal day to day activities or decisions. My behaviour has become so circumspect that whichever way I turn, I admonish myself for not having turned the other direction.

I no longer want to keep writing. The laughter next door is irritating and grating on my nerves. Why can't they just go to bed? Why does everything bother me so much? It's obvious.

My son is not here to talk to...

Day 56

I've lived long enough to have met countless number of elderly people and sometimes have listened to them repeat the same, sad story over and over again. This is not lack of memory on their part, but a sorrow so deep, that when they reach the end of their years, they recant this story, perhaps in hopes of reaching some clarity of understanding before they too, pass away.

I always thought it was so incredibly sad as I would listen to a parent mourn the loss of their child twenty, thirty, forty or even more years after the child had gone. I wondered at all the grieving parent held onto, deep in their soul, that never gave them any rest, never gave them any peace, never gave them any explanation for why their child is gone and they are left behind to stay and remember.

I used to surmise a pain as deep as that one is never rectified in a person's mind, or in their soul. Now, I am one of those parents and sometimes can't fathom living the rest of my life with this emptiness in my heart. Will I now become one of those babbling old women who will tell any passerby the story of her son? Many would say it will be my choice as to what I become, but I do feel some things are beyond our control. I do believe sometimes the pain is too vast, too broad, and too deep for a person to become anything else but an extension of the grief. I used to be in control of my mind, my thoughts and my emotions. Now, I no longer am and have mentioned before that I am doing things without any rational thought process and acting more from instinct than reason.

Just get the day over with as fast as you can. Just let there be no other dilemma come my way to deal with so I can bury deeper into myself and not have to explain, apologize or understand. Just let my life pass me by quickly so I don't become a lonely old woman whose mind has left her because she no longer can bear the pain of losing her son.

Someone told me that when good things start to happen in succession maybe I'll lose some of my fear and then won't be waiting for the next disaster to strike. I'm waiting for good things to happen, I really am, but I know right now that nothing can take away the sadness I feel and nothing can take away the shock I'm still in at having heard my son had died.

It was too much of a shock and I'm still reeling from the blow. I came in from a party and was still laughing as I picked up the ringing phone and heard the news my son was gone. How can this be? How can it be? I want to write different words in these chapters but I keep coming back to the same ones. How can it be? How can he be gone? How? How? How? Please, God, let it be a mistake. Let me not have joined the multitude of parents that have lost a child. This is a club I don't want to join. Let my child be alive and let me, God, have another chance to be a better parent.

I wasn't a good parent. I was always afraid and the more he tried to break away from my fear, the harder I tried to control and put the fear into him. I was so afraid for him that I don't think there was room for much else.

Do we know when something like this might happen to our child? Do we have some kind of premonition and want it so badly not to be? Is our life all set out before us and were they only to be here for a short time?

My doctor here in Mexico often talks about the child they lost in a car accident twenty years ago. The doctor says he has now set his life to help others, as if that explains the loss of his own child and somehow makes it make a semblance of sense. I want to scream at him that I would have done whatever was needed of me just not to have my child die. I see nothing good that can come out of this.

There were hundreds at his funeral and people came up to me, in hopes of cheering me up, saying, "Look how many people care about you that so many are here." I tell them I didn't need my son to die to know I had a lot of friends. It wasn't worth the price we had to pay.

Now, whatever comes into my life, nothing will ever make this ok. Nothing will ever make me think this or that may be the reason my son is gone. Why couldn't he stay?

Day 57

I would never assume to presume or presume to assume that God would change the weather expressly for me, but am starting to wonder. Last winter, when I was in Tucson, Arizona, they said it was the worst winter in a very long time. I thought the winter jacket packed for the trip down was not to be worn again until my sojourn back to Canada, but I was wrong. It was worn almost daily and while the weather in Canada was wonderful, Arizona could not make the same claim.

Not to worry, I say, because weather never affected me one way or the other. If it rained, somewhere a flower needed to grow, so my mood or attitude would never be changed by the change in the weather. My dad used to say that if it wasn't for the weather changing, ninety percent of the people would have nothing to talk about, and that always amused me to no end, because it was very true.

Now, here I am talking about, what else but the weather?

This winter in Arizona, friends are telling me it's warmer than usual and one of the best yet. I decide to go and tomorrow will be boarding a plane to Tucson to spend the New Year. Feeling mild trepidation, I'm also slightly excited, so have been checking out what to do and see in the city. On checking the weather for the upcoming week, it almost made me laugh when I saw they are expecting snow. It will arrive the same day I do, and leave the same day I leave. Com'n, God! Are you kidding me?

While I still would like to say that the weather doesn't affect my mood, I no longer can. The sunshine here in Mexico is a personal insult to the darkness inside. Yet I had hoped to do a lot of hiking up familiar mountain trails when I got to Tucson and now might be unable to do so. Whereas before, I would have found something else to amuse me, now I find myself not as flexible and unable to deviate from the simplest plan. The plan was to hike, the weather was to co-operate. The fact it didn't now leaves me befuddled and distressed. It is so hard to come up with a Plan A, please world don't make me also have to come up with a Plan B.

The minutest of tasks seems so incredibly insurmountable, and considering my circumstances, I'm doing the best I possibly can.

Tomorrow I leave Kelly the dog with my neighbors here and board a plane to Tucson. It will be slightly difficult to continue my writing from there, so will fill in the next six days upon my return.

It will also be the start of a whole new year next time I sit down to write. It will be 2011.

My son died in 2010. I wish I had, too...

Day 58 to Day 74

While it could be said this is a slightly unusual way to write a book, it would appear that now there is no rhyme or reason to anything I do. The last sixteen days have left me not wanting to write, so I didn't. Did I feel guilty? Yes. Did that change my mind and cause me to write? No.

Today I sat down at my computer and decided I wanted to write again. I know, down inside, it is the only purpose I have left in life, and for some reason, this is what I am now meant to do. Will my words ever mean anything to me? I don't know. Will my words ever mean anything to someone else? I certainly hope so.

My hope is that some other poor unfortunate, who finds themselves in my position of grieving their child, will be able to read my words, helter skelter that they may sometimes appear, and see themselves in the pain and anguish I am having such a difficult time conveying. I am hoping they too, will understand there are no words to properly explain the depth of my pain, for these are words that never should have been invented, and worse yet, ever used. The pain of losing your only child should be such an unthinkable, inconceivable occurrence that these words should never have been needed to be imagined or conceived.

So, what have the past sixteen days been for me? My plane set down on Arizona soil to the coldest cold I've felt in a very long time. Sleeting rain, blowing winds and the promise of ice storms soon had this sandal and summer outfit clad girl running for her winter jacket. For the duration of the next sixteen days, the winter jacket was never far away and thankfully, Brad loaned his sweatshirt for me to use.

Every time I make plans with him, I am nervous, for I am attached to this man I knew only a few short weeks before my son passed away. This man has now become someone of utmost importance and many times his words and reassurances make the day bearable. I am always afraid that if I care too much for someone or something, they will be taken away. Most of the time, my fears come to fruition, which further intensifies my fear.

Before I left for Tucson last winter, I had read The Alchemist by Paulo Ciehlo and he wrote, "Do not give in to your fears, for if you do, you cannot listen to your heart." I thought it was a wise saying and wrote it in bold letters on a piece of paper where it would always be forefront. I left that piece of paper beside my computer when I left Canada, and upon my return, when I heard my son was no longer with me, I tore the paper into shreds and threw it away.

All the wise sayings, all the words of wisdom, all the comfort, all the hope for tomorrow, all the dreams for the future, all the negation of the past, all the love yet to be explored and enjoyed; it all means nothing now.

He's gone. What can matter now? When I see my old personality peeking through wanting to please, wanting to do things fair and right and kindly, wanting to make the best of the day; when I see a glimmer of hope try to surface, I push it down and say "What is the use now?"

It makes me angry when someone says to me that I will love again, I will live again, I will laugh again, I will hope again. Tell me, you seekers of wisdom, how many children have you lost? If you have lost any, then I will listen. If not, walk away. Smile, wish me a reasonable day, for that is all I can hope for now, and just walk away.

I digress.

Brad met me at the airport and within seconds all my fears were gone. I don't want to lose what we have, and each time we are together, we grow closer. It is light and easy and fun and spontaneous being with him and I feel as though I'm with someone I have known a very long time. Is he like this with others and is it just his personality, or do we have a special bond? I want to think this is something special just the two of us have that he shares with no one else.

Is this love? I'm confused and afraid and grieving and so sometimes do think I am in love with him and know I would be devastated if he met someone else. We have talked about whether this friendship we have could grow into something stronger and I have to confess I'm afraid. Everyone I have ever loved has left, in one way or the other.

It makes me remember my mother often telling me, when I was a child, that no one would ever love me. She told me I was born unlovable and unlovable I would stay. Throughout my life I struggled and persevered to prove her wrong, but in the end, she was right. The only one I know for sure loved me was my son, and now he's gone, too. So, why would I even try to allow anyone to care about me, or worse yet, why would I allow myself to care? And yet care I do. I care for Brad and for so many others, but love has only ever caused me pain, my son's death being the worst imaginable; the worst possible. No one stays. They all leave.

Not death, God. Not death. Why couldn't he stay?

The time in Tucson, Arizona was wonderful. New Years Eve we went into the dessert and he kissed me at midnight. We were both so cold that seconds later we were huddled in his car and drove back home. It was good to be kissed by Brad at midnight. It was very, very good.

I came back to Mexico and Kelly the dog was very happy to see me. Since then we have continued to plod one foot in front of the other and go about our day. Every so often I see something interesting or do something interesting and think I need to write about it. But, when I sit down to write, it all seems so insignificant and of no intrinsic value, so quickly I forget what grabbed my attention for a millisecond.

Today is another beautiful, sunny day. I may lie down and watch television. Many times I now wonder where home is...

Day 75

I'm depressed. In fact, I'm in a deep, dark depression and can't claw my way out.

Today, my friends from Canada, Marcella and Bill, flew into Rincon de Guayabitos and we met for lunch. Marcella was my childhood friend and we had been each other's Maid of Honour at our respective weddings. As teenagers we would talk about how we would both marry wonderful men, live next door from each other, our children would play together and live happy lives.

While no life is trouble free, she basically got the dream while I got the nightmare, and soon her daughter will present Marcella and Bill with their second grandchild, something I now will never have.

We lost touch for around thirty years and when they heard what happened to my son, we reconnected. It was a terrible reason for an old friendship to bloom again, but both Marcella and Bill have since been very kind. While one part of me was greatly looking forward to seeing my old friend and her husband here in Mexico, the other part of me was frightened, for now I can't put on the happy for long without the sad coming at me like gangbusters. The sad overwhelms and overtakes and sucks me down into the mucky mire where I can't rise up. People don't stay with me in the muck and mire for long, and while I now feel a loneliness that is incomprehensible, I want to be surrounded by people who care about me and, could it be, love me.

I so desperately need to be loved and held and comforted that I'm like a throat parched woman dying of thirst, who will grab onto the slightest dribble of water. When anyone is kind, I gravitate towards them, but then don't want them to leave.

I feel that I belong nowhere, belong to no one, am adrift and lost in this sea of emptiness, am destined to be lonely the rest of my life, and the fear that grips my heart leaves me gasping for air and clutching at anyone and anything around me, just for someone or something to hold on to.

Who I belonged with was my son, and yet, did he ever feel he belonged with me? Did I continually push him harder, push him away, push him to be better, that maybe he felt he could never measure up? While I fault myself for every slight infraction in the raising of my child, there are some places where I truly did fail. And if he were alive, those failures would be minor and something to joke about. "Hey Mom, thanks for the years of therapy I'll be needing." And I would answer back with something equally as trite like, "Well, since I couldn't get you that pony you always wanted as a child, I knew I had to give you something."

God, I miss him.

Please, God, how do I survive?

Please, God, how do I go on?

I'm lost. I'm lost. I'm lost.

Day 76

I ended up spending most of yesterday with my friends and was happy to do so. Coming back to my empty apartment, the loneliness hit like a flashflood and I questioned whether it was easier to just remain alone and accept this is my fate, or to keep trying to be with friends hoping to feel slightly less alone?

I haven't come up with an answer and don't know that I will.

During the night my stomach was upset and I could feel that cold, achy feeling coming back. Today I arose feeling tired and sore and wondered if I would have to cancel plans for tonight. My neighbors down the hall have invited me to go hear a good musician play and I jumped at the chance for something to do tonight. The nights are the worst and the saddest and the loneliest, especially when I hear laughter from somewhere else. The laughter is like tiny shards of glass embedded in my soul. No matter which way I turn, the glass digs deeper and hurts more. There is no escape from what others would call the normalcy of life, and yet, I now find too difficult to bear.

While taking Kelly for her morning routine, I stopped in at Jan's to ask if they could Kellysit tonight while I went out. Before the question came out, I burst into tears and told her it was just a very bad day. This may have been the first time I've cried in front of her and she quickly got up to give me a hug. Kelly, who has taken on the role of my comforter, couldn't get at me as the table was to one side of me and Jan was standing up hugging me, to the other.

What did Kelly do? She went under Jan's caftan type nightgown and gave her a gentle goose. Jan shrieked and jumped, I kept crying, but when Jan said what happened, we both started to laugh. Trust Kelly. As I've said before, it's like she was given a job to do and she is doing it well.

I hate that she was given a job to do.

I don't hate that she is doing it well.

The rest of today was spent lying in bed with a sweater on and I am debating whether to go out or not. A wise woman would stay in bed and fight off whatever is fighting her. I no longer am a wise woman and have spent as much of this non vacation being sick in bed as was necessary.

Out I go...

Day 77

Last night was a sojourn into the Canadian party revelers version of Mexico. We went to a classy, upscale restaurant with English speaking Mexican waitresses and everyone seated in the packed restaurant were Canadian. I felt as if I was home, except my home is more humble.

It was an evening out and whereas before, I would have known many of the people and enjoyed kibbutzing and getting to know everyone, this time I sat quiet, struggling to find something to say. Intellectually I know I can't be sharing my bad news with everyone and yet little that anyone says to me matters any more. If they want to hear of my sorrow and listen to my sad plight, I feign a smidgeon of interest in the occurrences of their life; if they want to laugh and tell long, arduous, mundane stories, I have difficulty following, and notice I will ask the same question many times.

It is an effort in futility for me and why I ask the same question over and over is because I rarely listen to the answer people give. Nothing matters. It doesn't matter if the dress you bought is blue or grey, it doesn't matter if you went to the south of France or the North of England. It doesn't matter if you bought a house, sold a car, had duck for dinner, or any of the other nonsensical things that seem to make up the heart and soul of a human being and make their existence here on this unforgiving earth worthwhile.

How will I fit in now? I don't know, and would like to say I don't care. But, I think I do. I don't want to be sadder and I don't want anyone else to leave me or not like me or turn away from me or be angry with me. I already have beaten myself up to the ends of the earth and when I look in the mirror, see the face of a murderess who has murdered her own child. I didn't protect him enough when he was little. I didn't save him or shelter him from the cruelty of others, especially my family. I didn't provide for him, listen to him, encourage him, or know how to help him when he asked for advice.

The missing of my son is a longing that cannot find rest. I push it back, push it down, but sometimes it rises up and the pain of knowing this is not fixable or repairable or healable makes me want to lay down and die.

I pray every evening I will die.

I wake up every morning disappointed to be alive.

Why keep me here, God? You know I now will not do anything you require of me. You know I now have hatred and rebellion in my heart and you've brought me to my knees, but I won't let you lift me up. Why not put me out of my misery and let me go be with my son? Just let me go, God.

Tomorrow, my neighbor Jan and I, along with forty two other woman, are taking a bus trip to the city of Guadalahara. Jan asked if I would like to go and I said I would go, not caring one way or the other but just wanting to fill another day or two or three.

Today we all got an email from the coordinator saying it is zero degree weather during the day and colder at night. Once again I am going on a trip and taking my winter jacket along. Is it me, God? Is it me? I can't find any warmth anywhere and am sitting here in Mexico with my sweater and long pants on, and still cold.

Brad has booked his trip here and will be arriving in three weeks. I am nervous at how attached to him I am and sometimes want to push him away. I don't want to get too attached and then have him leave. It would be too heartbreaking to have more people I care about go away, but then somehow I wonder if this is not what I deserve.

I need to accept that being alone is what I deserve. I need to, but can't seem to. Last night I watched all the merry Canadians eating, drinking and listening to music in the restaurant we were at and wondered how it is I missed the boat. How is it I'm not one of those women celebrating many years of marriage, looking for gifts for her grandchildren, oblivious to the sorrow that comes from losing a child? How is it I failed at everything I've tried to do in my life? I know I'm intelligent and smart enough to figure things out. How is it I couldn't figure out how to make my life even a smidgeon successful? I think I would be ok with failing at everything else, but not with failing as a mother. I raised a child who, in the end, felt he had nowhere to turn.

Not even to me...

Day 78 to 81

The three days in Tonala, which is a suburb of Guadalahara, are over. Thankfully, the predicted nasty weather never did materialize, and we were all graced with warm sunshine and brighter days.

It was a shopping marathon, with forty six women in tow, happy to be on the loose and on the go. Laughter and merriment was in the air and I so hoped it would be contagious and rub off on me. It was not to be. I missed my son, thought of him constantly, and watching these women bemoan the fact they couldn't get their favorite knick knack in the color to match their kitchen, made me wonder how it was I missed it all? How did I miss even a semblance of normalcy and how was it that my dedication to pleasing others, with no thought of pleasing myself or my son, could have gone so wrong?

My roommate, Jan, found herself on the receiving end of much alcohol and proceeded to cause a scene at dinner our first night. Many ladies felt free to tell me how she spoiled the evening and they hoped this wasn't just a precursor of more to come, for we still had two more days to spend together. That night Jan slept soundly, presumably in the alcohol induced slumber, while I tossed and turned, unable to sleep, and feeling embarrassed for having come along. It could have happened to anyone, at any time, but now it seems that the slightest deviation from any plan, or the slightest glitch that may bring attention to me in a negative way, makes me unable to function.

Having lived through the sorrow of sorrows and the saddest of sad, I don't want a fingernail to break, for I feel that my sanity is barely holding on. If I lose it, what will become of me? Where will I turn? To whom will I turn to? I've felt this way for many years while my son was young, but relaxed somewhat as he grew to adulthood. Not that I had great expectations he would look after me, or that I would let myself be a burden to him, but it was simply a sense of belonging and someone to belong to. He and I, we were family. Now that he is gone, I feel adrift in a sea of faces, lost and alone.

Being with all these women the past three days made me realize, even more, that I have no entitlement to sharing my grief. I told one lady what happened and could see her uncomfortableness at hearing my news, so quickly changed the subject. She appeared relieved when I started talking about mundane, nonsensical subjects, thereby cushioning her from having to deal with my pain.

I found the three days grueling and am glad to be back to the safety of my small apartment and my loving dog. It is difficult to keep a smile pasted on my face and yet I don't know how much of the real me I can show. I just don't want any hassle. I don't want any more hardship. I don't want anything else to go wrong, no matter how minute.

I want to hold on to the tiny bit of reason and rationale I still have left.

Until God is merciful to me and answers my prayer to take me, I hope I can hang on.

Day 82

For all intents and purposes, today coulda, shoulda, woulda been a good day. This morning, Marcella, Bill and I rented a shuttle bus and went to the hot springs, where we basked and soaked until our skin was the texture of a prune. Totally satiated and relaxed by the mineral waters, we parted ways just after lunchtime and I proceeded to pick up my dog at my neighbors, Jan and her boyfriend. I can't say her boyfriend's name as it is the same name as my son, so would be too painful to write, to say, to feel or to think. It was a good name for a good boy who grew into a good man.

Why is he gone? He had so much potential. He had so many gifts. He had such a wonderful sense of humor and rarely did a phone conversation end without my peals of laughter ringing through my house. He was fun, my son. He was fun and funny and kind and caring and hard-working and good-looking and nice to be with. Why is he gone?

Why is he gone?

I can't bear he's gone.

Jan and her boyfriend invited me over for dinner tonight and that was an unexpected, pleasant surprise. Having a few hours to kill, Kelly the dog and I went up to the rooftop to tan.

Once the sufficient amount of sun rays had permeated my body, Kelly and I proceeded on to Jan's house. Supper was delicious, the conversation was fun, and it was a pleasant evening.

Nothing to complain about.

Other than I no longer have a living son.

Day 83

Today I have no agenda. I remember a song from my younger days that went, "Riding along in my automobile... no particular place to go", only difference being I have no automobile to be riding along in.

Basically, I fall into the category of "no particular place to go."

While I care deeply for my friends vacationing here from Canada, and want to spend as much time as possible with them, I find any activity extremely tiring. These past few days of having to find topics of conversation, all the while treading carefully to see how much of my grief they could bear, has left my mind exhausted and my spirit sore. I feel bruised and further wounded through no fault of anyone; it simply appears to be the state I now find my sorry self in, and if there is but a moment of respite from the sense of being sucked down into sorrow encased cement, I revel in the moment of calm.

It just seems I can't find those calm moments very often and don't know how to bring them about.

My head understands all the advice givers care about me and my wellbeing and want to see a turnabout from the sad, struggling to survive, person I've become. I do laugh, I do engage in trivial conversations, I do, many times, appear to be healing and healed and over it and under the grief radar, and back to myself. When people see me in these various states of normalcy, they smile and say, "See, we told you you'd be back to your old self in no time at all." To that ridiculous statement I feel like saying, "Yeah, it's not like he was important or anything, so really doesn't deserve to be missed or grieved much at all." The only problem with saying something like that is someone might totally misconstrue the sarcasm dripping statement and think I mean it. So, I'm very careful what I say and feel cheated because, at this juncture of my life, I shouldn't have to watch my words so carefully and would hope for more sympathy than I sometimes receive.

For the most part everyone has been kind, and maybe it's just me and my askew perception of things, but it's almost as if everyone, myself included, wishes this could be a nightmare that I've now woken up from and can continue being the person I used to be.

The best interpretation I can come up with is when someone has major surgery, you visit, commiserate, and mostly wait for the patient to recover. Once recovered, life goes on as it was before.

When someone loses their only child, you never recover, and life never goes on as it was before. For those waiting for me to be my old self, I would only assume there would be levels of frustration when I appear unfocused, forgetful, and sad.

The reason I appear that way is because I am.

Figure it out, people.

When I smile or laugh or talk about trivialities, I'm doing it mostly for you.

The only reason I'm doing it for me is because I don't want you to leave me.

Right now being alone is a very frightening place to be. Since I have no husband, no other children, and a very small family, my friends are who I turn to. Being in this amount of grief has somehow heightened my senses, and I have actually read and heard from other grieving parents that this is what happens when you lose someone. With these heightened senses, I can tell when you want to talk no heavies, laugh a little, or do something fun, so, like a chameleon, I follow along and change my mood to suit yours.

What ensues from the effort it now takes me to push away the grief is a day like today; a day where I feel physically, emotionally, spiritually, intellectually exhausted and combing my hair is a major effort. I will now back away from everyone and spend the day alone with my dog. If someone tries to engage me in conversation, I will have difficulty following their train of thought and will politely, but quickly, disengage. It is too tiring to continue and this grieving process produces a weariness, fatigue, apathy and lassitude beyond description. I exist in a state of torpor and find it increasingly difficult to shake off the lethargic indifference and lethargy.

As I've watched this pattern repeat itself, and know today will be spent avoiding people, I will be trying to grasp a mere resemblance of my former self, and when the loneliness sucks me down so low I can't bear it anymore, will paste on a smile and try again.

I don't know where to turn to let out this monumental amount of grief, so hold a lot of it in. Do I let it out when I'm alone? I'm afraid I won't be able to come back from it, and fear there will be no one to pick up the pieces if I completely unravel.

I miss my son.

I have never felt so alone.

And wonder if this is how he must have felt?

Day 84

Last night my downstairs neighbor, Edith, and I decided to try our hand at belly dancing. The lessons were fun and a vigorous workout was had by all. It would appear, to all intents and purposes, that I am having a lot of fun, and if it weren't for the fact I am mourning my only child, I would be.

Because of my circumstance, fun is no longer a word I would use in my vocabulary. What I am doing now is enduring, hoping for time to pass quickly so the pain would subside. What I am now doing, instead of looking towards the future for a better tomorrow, is wanting my life to pass by in a blur and a hurry and am merely existing, waiting to die.

What a senseless, useless existence this is. I've talked to other grieving parents and they say that once they lost their child, they have to keep constantly busy and never stop. That is the only way they can deal with the pain. To me, that too, is a senseless existence, willing the time to pass by quickly so our life could be over.

I would rather my life be over now.

Why wait? What am I waiting for?

People say I will find a reason for being, there will be a purpose for my life and I need to watch and wait for it to unfold.

News flash, people.

I don't want it to unfold.

I don't want to feel what I'm feeling right now.

I don't want to wait for a better tomorrow.

My son never got a better tomorrow.

Why should I?

Do I sometimes repeat myself in these writings, musings and diatribes I endeavour to accomplish every day?

I probably do.

Could it be because I care for so little now?

I have only questions and no answers.

And for now, that will have to do.

Day 85

I'm spitting mad and of course, only this blank page I'm typing on will ever know about it. Why am I mad? Well, let me tell you. Most of my life people have felt a freedom to say when they are unhappy with anything I say, do, feel, or think, and I, on the other hand, have never opened my mouth to speak my mind.

When someone hurts my feelings or does anything untoward, I keep quiet and let it go until it goes away. Others don't feel the same way.

So, while I love my friends dearly and would leave none of them out of my life, sometimes their comfortableness to tell me what they think, and also their security that I won't get offended or upset, leaves me wanting to run away and hide.

Or maybe it's not security in our relationship they feel. Maybe its indifference and they are not as attached to the friendship as I am, so are willing to take a chance the friendship could end.

I'm not that confident and am afraid to lose more people in my life, so as I've done in the past, keep my thoughts to myself and explain away or apologize for any hurts, real or imagined, that I may have caused.

It didn't matter so much before. Now, it matters. Now, the passive, agreeable, always smiley person I used to be is someone I detest. She smiled her way through many hardships and didn't deal with the reality of how her son must have been feeling. She taught him to smile and not speak up when he was hurting, but rather to shove it all inside, until he couldn't shove any more in. She taught him they were throwaway people that didn't matter too much, and others desires were more important.

She taught him wrong.

And now he's gone.

And still she smiles her way through this terribleness and sadness, all the while feeling the bile rise up.

Why am I so afraid?

I am so afraid to be what I am; alone.

The more frightened I am and the harder I try to please, the more alone I am.

I have little extended family, no immediate family, no financial security, poor health, nowhere I feel to completely break down and let loose, and am now grieving my only child, who was so broken hearted he couldn't see a way out other than suicide.

I am undone.

And still I smile and let trivialities pass by.

And still I don't show my grief because I don't want the other person to be uncomfortable.

And I guess now, it doesn't much matter. But, I'm still afraid.

And I wonder if this is how my son felt. It breaks my heart and the tears don't help.

Where do I turn? I turned to God and there was no comfort. I turned to friends and they try to, but can't fully understand. The few that do say words that are like salve to my soul, I cling to, and want to be with them all the time. The intellectual part of me understands that isn't possible, but a small, childlike need, deep inside me, wants someone to just take over and look after me.

My friend came over yesterday and I asked her if she would like to take a cab here one evening and go belly dancing with me. At first she thought it was a good idea and then said she wouldn't because she wasn't ready to take a cab by herself for she wasn't brave like me. Throughout our friendship, she's made comments as to my independence and how able and capable I am. Because she wasn't, she then got a man who looks after her and worries about the details. I remained able and capable and now am too tired and befuddled to look after myself, but who is there to do it for me?

This time her comment stung. I said nothing, but later thought of all the things I should have said. The principal one being, "Aren't you lucky you don't have to be brave like me?", but of course, I would never say it.

Why would I never say it?

Because this is a wonderful friend who probably would apologize for offending me in any way, and I am afraid to take the chance to say anything that might hurt her. I am just afraid.

And tired...

So tired...

So tired of life...

So tired of living...

So tired of struggle...

So tired of pain...

God, please take me to be with my son.

Day 86

It would appear grieving parents, or at least this grieving parent, can't deviate from routines and need to establish them quickly or nothing gets done. I get up, get dressed, make the bed and press the button for the coffee to brew. God help me if I've forgotten to make the coffee the night before for it puts me into a panic and throws my entire pattern off.

While the coffee is brewing, I brush my teeth, wash my face, make my breakfast, sit myself down at my computer and either check my emails or write and then take the dog for her morning walk. Depending on how I've slept the night before, this usually takes me into the afternoon, which is spent either lying in bed watching TV, sun tanning on the rooftop, or walking the avenida with my perro.

The first few months in Mexico, while being sick and all, evenings were spent huddled in my bed, watching the few English speaking channels I have, or reading a book. Mostly they were spent crying, or trying not to.

I've lost my son, world. How are you expecting me to function day to day? I barely have the capacity to look after myself and yet sometimes feel I also have to look after you.

People are offended if my tone sounds curt. I don't mean to be; it's just that whatever you are finding so important is so insignificant to me. People are offended if they haven't seen me or heard from me for a while. Then, don't come at me offensively; come at me asking if I'm coping and do I need someone there beside me while I cry. People come at me upset with their minuscule, minute, insignificant, menial dilemmas and want me to help or listen or empathize. I understand that to you these are the issues monumental in your life. I understand. I understand. I understand.

But please understand that I can barely function through the day, paste on a smile that actually causes me pain so that you are not uncomfortable with me, and only function in "yes" and "no". Everything in between is simply white noise and I lose you. I lose what you are trying to say and I see your frustration with me in not remembering what you may have said but a moment ago.

Many friends tell me not to paste on the smile and to be honest with people about how I feel. So I try it with the very person who is giving me such sage advice. Within moments they have an appointment they forgot about, or someone waiting they'd neglected to mention, or any other plausible excuse, and I'm left further frustrated because I opened up the ocean of emotions that are swirling inside, and then am left with these emotions taunting me as to how alone I really am.

I know some friends, reading this, will be offended at my honesty, and best I can say to that is you probably are not who I'm thinking of when I'm writing this. Why do I feel a need to even say that? Why can't I trust my friendships are strong enough that people will understand and not leave me? Why am I repeatedly apologizing and explaining myself at a time when others should be comforting me?

Because I am no longer sure anyone will stay behind. My son didn't.

We all have worries and fears and sad thoughts, but most times they never come to fruition. All of my worries, fears and sad thoughts have come about and more. Would you not be afraid, too?

Yesterday was a very sad day for me and I found myself exhausted by people and their tiny demands on my time.

When I feel like that I need to back away from everyone and hibernate, which is what I did. Most of the afternoon and evening was spent in bed and I sorely missed my son. I understand other grieving parents when they tell me they have to keep continually busy for if they don't, the missing of their child becomes paramount in their lives and they can't function to move on.

When I have a day like yesterday all I do is think of his life with me and how many places I failed him. I've always been the sort of person where things had to make sense. A plus B had to equal C and I couldn't deviate from finding the reason and the cause for various circumstances, whatever they may be.

Still the only answer I can come up with that makes this even the tiniest bit plausible is I'm to blame. I'm to blame for the sadness and sorrow in his life and I'm to blame for him having to make the choice he made. I'm to blame and I deserve this living death. To take me to be with my son would be too merciful and no punishment so God must feel I need to be punished here on earth for my terrible sin. I caused my child to die.

With thoughts like those, there is no escape. There is nowhere to turn. There is no relief from the grief. There is no other emotion but to mourn. With thoughts like those, my downward spiral into nothingness is what I feel I deserve.

I email with a wonderful lady who has lost two children. A mutual friend connected us and I've only met her once, but we are sisters in our grief. A few days ago I apologized for telling her how I really feel, which is that I want to die, and don't want to try, and yesterday I received an email back from her saying to never apologize. She said it takes courage to tell the truth about how I'm truly feeling and I need not apologize for my honesty. She is like salve to my wounded soul, but I need to hear those words over and over again for like a well-worn pathway, my negativity creeps in, and lays down in my mind like a comfortable dog.

That was my evening last night; one where I couldn't find comfort until the sweet oblivion brought about by many sleeping pills. At about 2 a.m. I woke with a start and felt someone whispering in my ear, "You were a good mother." Startled and confused, for I was alone in the room, I tried to whisper those words, thinking maybe I had said them in my sleep. No matter how I tried to emulate the sound and the words, the proper inflection would not come. Someone else had said those words.

I felt it was my son. I also felt he wanted to say more but I became afraid.

Some may think I've imagined all this, but as a grieving mother, I find I go more by instinct than logic or reason. I also find I'm closer to the other world and this world seems so trivial, so irrelevant, and there is so much ado about nothing.

Before this happened to me, I would hear other people talk about experiences they'd had, and must admit to being the biggest of scoffers. I believed in God and heaven and that there was more to life than this paltry existence, but some of the things people said happened to them, I found difficult to believe.

I even find this difficult to believe.

The one thing I do feel is sad, for even in death, once again, my son is comforting me.

I was never there enough for him.

I never comforted him when he needed to be.

I was so afraid to lose him that I tried to not love him too much.

I failed at that.

I loved him too much, so much.

Hopefully when I'm done beating myself up this go around, I will remember and grasp on to those few words whispered to me in the night.

"You were a good mother."

Day 87

I was going to write in a different direction today and hurried to open up my computer so I could start. With the words fresh in my mindless mind, that now forgets things one second after she sees them, hears them, speaks them or thinks them, I was anxious to get the words out before they left me, never to return. However, my original thoughts for this chapter were not to be.

Spelling is a big personal peeve of mine and I'm always very quick to zone in on misspelled words in books I read, so when writing my chapters, I go on the internet and have dictionary.com handy.

Upon opening the homepage to my internet site, there was a picture of the most popular destination Canadians move to, and how this particular city has now become the "it" place to live and to be. Without reading the destination name, I knew what it was, and actually have been on the very spot the picture was taken when driving to see my son in his hometown of Calgary.

Calgary, Alberta has now become the city many flock to and was where my young son moved to when he was still a teen. He had high hopes, big dreams, and good wishes from his mom.

He had little else and within days had not one, but two jobs, and was on his way. My child worked tirelessly and without complaint and while I knew he worked hard, I don't think I allowed myself to fully comprehend how hard.

He took menial jobs, difficult jobs, jobs other people wouldn't do. He worked construction and tried to put himself through school to be a mechanic. As he was also working a full time job, he decided on a different pathway, and took an apprenticeship to be a carpenter.

He was a good carpenter. He was a good worker. He was someone you could rely on and trust. Various employers kept trying to make him foreman and it became a joke during our telephone calls. He'd say he just started working for such and such and I'd say, "It has been three days since you started. Are you foreman yet?" He never wanted to be a foreman and was quite content being the worker bee, for whatever he did, he did well.

I can't write this.

It is too difficult to write.

I've been running away from my memories and thoughts of him and feel I could never do justice to chronicle and accurately recount the wonderful person he was. He got a raw deal. He never got a chance to be all he could be. He worked so hard, too hard, and couldn't do it anymore.

I feel I must finish the reason I started writing about Calgary although now my words have lost me and my body is shaking. I know I am desperately trying not to feel the pain I must feel to heal. When I allow myself to think of my son as he was, everything in me shakes and tremors and I become so afraid; so afraid to live on this earth without him.

How do I go on when I so desperately don't want to?

My son ended up buying a house in Calgary and it was a wonderful home. You could see his pride in his achievement and when I would visit him there, I would marvel at all he had done. He worked hard, too hard. That home meant a lot to him and we thought the reason he had done what he did was because he was losing his home. He wasn't. He had made a payment the month he died but he had no money to make any more.

Now his home, and I still think of it as "his", is lost. I couldn't keep up the payments and why would I, even if I could? It was the house my son died in. Going there probably wouldn't be a good idea, although when I first heard the news, my thoughts were to sell my place and go live in my son's house. It was an irrational thought, of which I had many, but in my mind, it was somehow going to bring me closer to him. If I could live in his house, I would just wait for him and we would laugh at what a huge colossal mistake this all was.

In his quiet, shy, dry humor way, my son would say, "Yeah, it would really suck to be the guy who did die. Glad it wasn't me."

That is what I was waiting for and think I still am. Being here in Mexico, which is a place he's never been so it doesn't always feel like he's gone. Those are the days I can laugh and be social. Days like the past two I've spent alone, the reality is that he's gone, and won't be there for me to call.

Now his house has been repossessed by the mortgage company and someone else will live in it. They will hear the sad story that the previous owner shot himself in this house, and maybe take a moment to feel sad, but then the excitement of owning this home and probably getting it at a good price will take over any thought of the previous owner.

They will never know he had a name, and a life, and a career, and friends, and hope and a desire for love, and an amazing sense of humor, and so many other attributes; too numerous to mention.

They will never know he had a mother who loved him, who will mourn him all the days of her life.

Neither will they care...

Day 88

I feel very grumpy today. I feel very lost and alone and sad and mournful and generally dissatisfied with my lot in life.

Yesterday I met my friends from Canada for dinner here in La Penita, at a restaurant that used to have Karaoke but now no longer does, much to our chagrin. I was the first to arrive and thought I would watch the sunset all the while watching for them from the corner of my eye.

The sunset was more amazing than I envisioned and made me long for a life as beautiful as this world sometimes was. I stood there watching the clouds turn a bright crimson, hoping to be awed by God's artistry, and yet none of the beauty found its way inside my heart.

As I stood there, I wondered how it was I missed everything in life. I missed having a loving family to protect and care about me, I missed having a husband to grow old and comfortable with, I missed financial stability and all the trimmings in life that came with it, but most of all, I missed leaving this earth before my child. That is the saddest miss of all and the knowledge I will never watch him give me grandchildren or attain all the dreams he had in his life causes a pain that is, once again, beyond explanation.

So, today I feel grumpy and sad and hate that I have to waste the days feeling like this. I hate that my life and my son's life couldn't have been a success and a life where we overcame. Instead the sadness and perils of life overcame us and now I don't know what else to do but be sad. I told my friends at dinner last night that I now don't know how to be. They were kind but also said people, including themselves, didn't know how to be with me, and were relieved when I put on the happy face and pretended nothing was wrong. I understand, and it seems too often now, I am put in a position where I have to understand.

As I stood watching the sunset, I willed it to go down faster for I was concerned my friends might be waiting and I didn't want to be late. Behind me a woman I'd never met was also watching the sunset and we started to converse. Telling her I had to keep one eye watching for my friends as I didn't want to be late, she asked what would be wrong if I was. The question took me off balance and I had no good answer for she was speaking the truth. What is this terrible need I have to please and please and please? And further, why did I try and make my son the same?

What would have been wrong if I was late?

Standing there further watching the sun fall beneath the sky, I asked God how it was I missed it all; this god I no longer think much of but yet miss having a daily conversation with. As I've spent so much time alone in my life, God had become a friend of sorts and I talked to him all the time. Now it would seem I talk to Kelly the dog and yesterday told her she is around so I don't look like a crazy old lady talking to herself. Kelly the dog seemed to concur.

Back to God. Still standing, now immersed in the sunset and yet feeling only sorrow in my heart, the only answer to my question came as one word. The word was "fear". I lived in fear most of my life, and now live in it even more. And yet, what more can be taken from me? I have little left to lose, and if I were to lose my life, the only emotion would be gratitude that I no longer have to stay. I say that now, but if something were to happen, I know I would also feel fear, for it has become a sadly comfortable emotion that is like an old friend; one you wish wouldn't be so close, but you do nothing to push away.

As I write this I think what does anything matter anymore? Nothing matters, why do I still try and search for answers in a world that has given me only pain. While I will take some of the blame I won't take it all. There were sorrows that happened to me which I never feared at all. They were too horrible to think about and only after they happened, did the fear materialize.

It's not fair.

It's not right.

I'm grumpy and irritable and don't see how to claw my way out.

I'm mad at everyone who have their children and while I want these people to go away, I don't want to be alone.

How do I get to a place in my life where alone is okay?

I don't know.

Day 89

Usually I write in the mornings and then go on with my day. Today, Marcella and Bill invited me to go on a whale watching tour and then to a small island where they would go snorkeling and I could suntan or explore.

First I said yes I would go, then I had a few sad, weepy days where I doubted my ability to laugh and smile, so then I said no, then I said yes again, then I said no. Since my new found life without my son has begun, I've grown increasingly anxious about the smallest decision and everything has become a colossal undertaking. I vacillate constantly, and second guess any decision I make. The reason for this is mostly I don't trust my own emotions and don't want to inconvenience anyone with my uncontrollable tears.

Minutes before I was to meet them, after a resounding no last night, I decided yes I would go. Rushing to take Kelly to the dog sitters, I briskly walked the mile to meet my friends. They were both surprised to see me, but took it in stride, and since I keep forgetting I'm in Mexico where no one is on time we proceeded to wait another hour before the boat took us out.

Heading towards the open ocean in search of whales, I sat at the front of the boat where no one could see my tears. They flowed freely and holding them back became a difficult process. If anyone noticed, no one said.

I was sorry I had gone, for I found no joy anywhere, not even when we saw the whales.

I missed my son.

I hurt for my son.

I ached to be with my son.

I couldn't find peace.

Later, Marcella and I walked the beach, with Bill trailing behind, and I tried to talk to her about how afraid I was to lose more people in my life, and since who I mostly had were friends, I hid away until I felt strong enough to be out in public again.

She thought it was a bad idea for me to spend so much time alone, but when I asked if she would be comfortable with my crying all the time, she agreed she wouldn't.

I told her I felt trapped.

She told me I'd spent too much of my life worrying about other people and what they thought and how they felt.

She told me, maybe now, it was time to start thinking about myself.

I told her I didn't know how.

Day 90

It has been ninety days I've now been here; ninety days since I left Canadian soil. I don't want to go back. I don't want to stay here. I don't know what I want.

What I have come to realize is I agree with all the other grieving parents I've met in that I need to stay busy. The few friends I have here sometimes get offended that I don't want to come over and sit. Sit and visit. Visit and sit. Since most of my life has been spent careful to avoid offending everyone, I try to come to my point from different angles and say, when I sit and visit, the "sad" sits and visits, too.

The "sad" then wants to cry, scream, yell, or numb itself in any way possible because when I sit and visit, the "sad" grows.

Few understand.

Those who do understand seem to comprehend so much more of what I'm going through and for them I will be eternally grateful. While I would like to forever immortalize them by writing their names on paper, I wouldn't do so, for they are also the type of people who wouldn't want to be praised for their kindness.

I hope, in some way, I have let you know who you are.

Today is a busy day with many things on my agenda. These are not fun things to do, but rather business type things like banking, and my mind feels overwhelmed. My friend told me yesterday, while she and I were basking in the sun on the little island, her husband was information gathering for their next outing, that he looks after things and is the organizer. I told her she was very lucky because I've always had to look after things and especially right now, wish someone would just take over and let me grieve.

I wish I didn't have any responsibilities and could go hide away, still knowing someone is in the next room, and will be there to care once I'm over the next wave of pain.

Marcella said, in life, we sometimes get what we are most afraid of and when we entertain fears, we bring them about. I've heard that said many times, in different ways, and the very idea puts such fear into my heart as to make me feel immobilized.

That would mean I brought about my son's death because I was so afraid. That would mean I brought about my aloneness and my sorrow and my pain.

If that were true, then that means I could bring about my death, for if a principle works in one way then it should work in the other. What I feared for my life has come about but not because I wanted it to. Rather, I so desperately didn't want it to, and felt I was racing against time, wanting to come to the end of my days, still unscathed, still knowing only a certain amount of sorrow.

I wanted the end of my days to come with my son saying goodbye to me and not the opposite.

This was difficult to write, this was difficult to think, this is a difficult life to live.

Day 91

Today I'm deciding whether to go home at my scheduled time, end of February, or stay till the middle of April. The only reason I was going home early is to do a one year memorial for my son, as Russian tradition does a mini funeral service of sorts and it is a sign of respect to the departed.

When planning this trip, a friend said I can show my respect to my son while I'm somewhere else, but, at that time the idea of not doing this one year memorial was unthinkable.

Now, I am afraid.

I am afraid to go home. I am afraid to do a mini funeral service. I am afraid to come back to the memories. I am more afraid now to face the truth of his passing than I was before I left. Then, it was all new and surreal. Now, it has grown old and real.

I still sense I have not fully grieved. I still sense I'm holding in a grief so monumental, so gargantuan, as to be immeasurable. If I let it out, will I totally lose my mind?

Will I sink into a deep, dark abyss there will be no coming back from? Will I merely cease to exist, but for my body continuing to function on this unforgiving earth?

I never want to go home, for I fear it may be my undoing.

If everything I've ever feared has come about, and it has, even the unthinkable, it would only stand to reason this last fear of losing my mind is next.

What a detestable, deplorable, disgusting thought. And yet it is my thought, and pushing it away with all my strength only seems to cause it to become stronger.

I've known the effects of mental illness. My mother was mentally ill and lived in a world she created, full of delusions, hallucinations and paranoia. She believed her make believe world was more real than the world she truthfully lived in, and I've often said your reality is how you perceive things and not necessarily how they really are. She caused my son and me a lifetime of suffering and torment and many times I would wish and pray for her sanity to be restored. It was not to be.

If only she had created a world of beauty. We would all be the better for it. That also was not meant to be.

Having come from that family background and suffering the repercussions of her insanity, my lifelong quest was to remain sane. Many people have told me it is remarkable I never turned to drugs, or alcoholism, or ran from therapist to therapist in my quest to undo the damage my mother had done.

She was very famous, and not in a good way, in our small town, and was widely known as Crazy Anna. I, then, was also known as Crazy Anna's daughter and fought to negate the stigma caused by this label my entire life. I kept my proverbial nose clean and would sometimes say, "If anyone has anything bad to say about me, it will never be the truth. I will be a woman without any guile." Thus set about my further quest for perfection. For, in my mind, if I could only be perfect, nothing worse could happen and we would be loved.

It was a quest without end and one where I could only fail.

The biggest regret is I taught my son the same values and taught him he couldn't fail.

He didn't.

I did.

When asked why I exerted so much energy trying to live the best life I could live, in spite of harrowing, heart-breaking circumstances, I would always say, "I have a son," and knew no further explanation was needed.

Now I don't.

I am now free to die.

What a terrible legacy.

Did I cause him to make this terrible decision, or am I just looking for more ways to punish myself and cause myself the pain he must have felt?

Am I looking to sink lower, lower, lower, until I make the same decision my son made?

Am I hoping to overcome my fear of taking my own life and finding ways to make living so excruciatingly unbearable that I can't take it anymore?

Am I looking to drive myself to either taking my own life, or losing my mind, in order that I no longer have to feel?

Am I searching for any escape from this burden I now bear?

I think I am...

Day 92

Yesterday I changed my flight to go home April 18, 2011; one day after I buried my son and one day before my birthday. I hope packing up to leave Mexico will leave me too busy to let April 17th take me over, and instead, somehow the day will go by.

Did I make the right decision? I'm not even thinking about it and it doesn't much matter; I just know I'm afraid to go home.

This morning I woke cold and tired and I didn't want to get out of bed. On days like these I bring Kelly into bed with me and she snuggles close, giving me comfort. Sometimes I get annoyed because I have to look after her and then I feel so incredibly guilty. Somewhere in life I gave up my free will that allowed me to be human and make mistakes. Somewhere in life I forgot to learn I could be forgiven. Somewhere in life I lost perspective on any importance or value I may have.

Somewhere in life I struggled for a purpose when I needed to just relax and be me.

Somewhere in life I never learned who I was or what I was meant to accomplish.

I merely wanted to become invisible to the world so no more cruelty could find me.

It found me anyways, in the saddest of forms.

Now who do I become?

I only want my son.

Lying in bed for hours, this morning made me feel more morose and despondent. Forcing myself to get up only when I got too hungry to stay in bed, I proceeded to the kitchen area and made myself a cheese omelette, two slices of unbuttered toast, sliced tomato and avocado and then I devoured the feast.

Immediately upon eating, I felt better. Instantly my mood lifted.

Could I have something as simple as low or high blood sugar? While it couldn't be blamed entirely for my depression, it could be a contributing factor.

Or have I simply become a foodaholic and am trying to feed the inner gnawing within that will not give me rest?

It matters little.

Today will be another Nina and Kelly the dog day, hiding away...

Day 93

Today was a busy day. In the morning my neighbor, Jan, and I went to the market while Kelly stayed behind with Jan's boyfriend. It was the first time I've been to the market without Kelly and it was fun to just look at clothes, meander through the busy market, and basically not feel a rush to be somewhere by a certain time.

It was a good morning.

Jan and I parted ways and I went home to wait for my friend, Marcella. I hadn't seen my friends from Canada for a while and found I missed being with someone familiar, who knew me before, with whom I felt comfortable enough to sometimes just be me.

Whenever I'm with Marcella I want to cry and let my guard down because she is a place of comfort for me. Logically, I understand she is here on vacation and doesn't want to hear my cries or see my tears, but illogically, which is a state I would rather exist in, I want to cry and have her hug me.

Today we walked the beach from La Penita to Guayabitos and when we got to her hotel room, I started to cry. She was telling me the story of how she made gifts for the entire graduating class where her son had graduated from, and I thought about my son, who had been to ten schools by the time he was in the ninth grade. I thought of his life and how afraid I was that someday he would do what he did.

It was as if I was willing the time to pass by quickly so I could grow old and die, and still have him safe on this earth, hopefully having conquered all the obstacles that came his way.

It was not to be.

And today I needed to cry.

As I was telling Marcella I didn't want to live in a world where my son no longer was, her husband walked in.

Quickly my tears dried up, I donned my sunglasses to hide the residual hint of my tears, and conversation turned to where we wanted to go for dinner.

The moment was over.

I need those moments.

Whom do I have them with?

I need someone to hold me while I cry.

And I so desperately need to cry...

Day 94

I woke up after only a few hours of sleep and couldn't journey back to the land of slumber without more medication.

In the best of times, a sleepless night produces lethargy, irritability, and greatly lessens an individual's quality of life; or is it only one's perception of their quality of life?

Whatever it was, I could not hang onto even a mere smidgeon of gratitude for my state of being, and upon getting up, found that my sleepless, gnarly state was further intensified by aches and pains throughout my body.

It would appear I overdid yesterday and now wonder about pursuing any activities today. When I sit and do little, the negative thoughts are paramount and I grapple and struggle for a reason to go on. I really have none, and the few glimmers of sunshine in my life are quickly further negated on a day like today.

An old back injury and subsequent misalignments by a physiotherapist have left me cautious and careful when dealing with my back. A wrong movement can bring on a headache of gargantuan proportions and further treatments have never improved my condition.

Now, it would appear I can't return to belly dancing classes, at least not tonight, and it frustrates me that a simple pleasure is not to be.

I feel like whining today. Maybe I should stop writing.

I sometimes wonder if I'm writing for me or for you. If there never is any "you" reading this, then do I need to continue writing? Does it benefit me much at all? I don't know, for I appear to exist in this nothingness where I don't much care what helps and what doesn't. And yet I do. I want comfort, I want caring, I want love, I want to feel I belong somewhere, but most of all, I want my son.

Or more yet, I want to go where he is.

Don't make me stay, God.

So I continue to write in hopes I will feel somehow necessary, somehow worthwhile, somehow needed in this world I've never felt I belonged in. I continue writing thinking someday someone, who has experienced what I've experienced, will gain insight into what they are feeling by reading my words. I continue to write in hopes that whoever that someone reading my words will be, that they will come to understand they are not losing their mind, just as I know I'm not losing mine. I continue to write hoping they will see themselves in me and know it is the grief, the all-encompassing, deplorable, hateful, hurtful, vengeful grief that makes it appear we are not normal.

We're not.

Day 95

Yesterday was a day spent in bed trying to keep warm, all the while holding back tears. It was a day where I could see my son's face clearly, in my mind's eye, and I ached for him. I longed just to hear his voice, see his whimsical smile, and laugh at his dry, witty sense of humor.

I can't bear this longing and wanting him to be alive. I can't bear the thought he's gone. I can't bear he was so unhappy that he saw this as the only way out.

Do other parents make mistakes in the raising of their children? Do other parents regret a lot of decisions they may have made or not made? Do other parents then lose their children? Why did this happen? Why did it happen to him?

When he was a baby, I thought he was so perfect. Having been raised in a family where I was shown little caring and taught how imperfect I was, I was afraid some of my imperfections would rub off on this beautiful child. I didn't know how to guard and protect him and thought he was too precious to make a mistake with, so what did I do? I did nothing. I made few decisions. I guided him very little, and left him to make his own way.

I sorely regret those decisions and see how very difficult it was for him to make his own way with no family support of any kind.

Today I am angry at my family. I'm angry at my brothers for being hateful and cruel. I'm angry at my dad for taking the path of least resistance, like I did, and doing nothing to protect this child from harm. I'm angry at my crazy mother, who we spent my son's entire childhood running from. I'm angry at extended family for caring more about their comfort than the safety of this little boy. I'm angry at my ex-husband who just walked away without a moment's concern. I'm angry at myself for the choices I made and for thinking I had to make my son strong, instead of safe.

I'm angry.

What purpose is my anger?

No purpose at all.

I'm also angry at friends who should be supporting me right now and instead are concerned about themselves. I'm angry that I still have to defend myself and put up with other's foibles because of my deep fear of being alone. I'm angry that I let things go and don't sweat the small stuff, but so many don't let go things I do or say.

I'm angry I can't find anywhere where I feel safe enough to completely break down. I'm even angry at my dog because she is a responsibility.

What would I do if she wasn't around?

I would wither and quiver in my bed, and never get up.

Day 96

Today was an incredibly exhausting day. I have been having such terrible night's sleep and am awake early in the morning, struggling to get back to sleep, for that is when the mind is most furtive and refuses to let you rest. Even if you have nothing substantial to keep you awake, the mind still plays tricks on your seemingly blasé life and you question things in the darkness you would never even ponder in the day.

To be living my nightmare and to awaken in the middle of the night is despondency and despair beyond description.

I seem to have a lot of feelings that are beyond description. They should never have had to be described, lived through, or felt.

This has been a succession of days without sleep and last night's consisted of a dream where I could not breathe. Gasping for breath and beseeching my friends to help me, for I felt surely I would suffocate, I awoke, still clutching for air. It frightened me so terribly that sleep was now to be non-existent. Turning on the television frustrated me more because there was only murder, mayhem and despair, and I didn't even try to read as the frustration level I felt made concentration impossible.

Rising to go to the washroom, my legs were unsteady and the realization hit me I was still under the effects of the sleeping pills taken but a few hours before. Taking more would be pointless, or maybe it would bring about the demise I so desperately covet and seek.

Feeling the cold of the night air in this unheated apartment and watching the sun rise brought about no warmth to my body or my soul. I seem to be cold all the time now and don't have a gauge to know if it's simply me or if it truly is cold outside. Unfortunately, right now in Mexico, it really is cold outside, and sometimes the chill permeates my body and I cannot get warm.

Mid-morning found me tossing and turning, and finally, I got up.

Shortly after taking Kelly for her by now early afternoon walk, my friend knocked on the door. She was unexpected as we had no plans for today but I was happy to see her.

I so desperately needed to talk and once the floodgates opened, the words rushed out and it was difficult for me to stop. I let the tears flow and sometimes felt this need to back down a little because I didn't want to overwhelm her, but I so needed to talk. The words ran wild, unabated and seemingly with a will of their own.

I needed to talk.

I needed to cry.

I needed someone to still be there when I stopped.

I couldn't seem to stop.

I'm searching for answers in a world where there exist only questions.

Telling story after story of the life my son and I led, left my friend shocked and horrified, and when I said that my son didn't stand a chance after the horrific life he led, she didn't disagree.

It broke my heart.

I wanted him to be the exception to the rule.

I didn't want to believe in a world of cause and effect, for then we were doomed.

I wanted us to overcome and be a success story.

I thought we were.

I was wrong, and don't know how to live with myself.

I have no energy left to continue to try.

Nor do I want to...

Day 97

You would think having a day of crying preceded by many sleepless nights would bring about exhaustion so monumental as to render me semi-comatose for many hours. You would think, but it was not meant to be.

Emotionally, mentally, physically, spiritually exhausted I went to bed around 10 p.m. Once I took my maximum allowable dosage of sleeping pills, sleep came quickly like a thief in the night. I don't remember falling asleep.

I do remember waking up. Looking at the clock sitting on my nightstand, the numbers read 4 a.m. Rubbing the sleep from my eyes in hopes I hadn't seen the time clearly, the clock still showed the time at 4 a.m.

And that would be that. If we were to believe the fables we've heard along the way, there was no more "sleep for this wicked", for that must be how I see myself and feel I am.

Talking to my friend all those hours showed me the fruitlessness of pursuing a happy life for myself and my child. It showed me that when I had reached my quota of how much sadness I could watch my child live through, I simply shut down and my entire being could take no more. I couldn't bear to see him hurting anymore and so pretended nothing was wrong.

He was the epitome of a storybook child, one who never complained, loved his mother, and treated people with kindness. I thought we had beaten the odds and all the pain in his life had not brought him down.

I was wrong.

We were victims of circumstances and products of our torturous upbringing and no one, not even God, could save us.

We were doomed to die; one physically, one in every way except her body closing down.

If I had more sleep, would I be writing a different chapter today? I don't know, but know that it no longer matters what words spew forth. My son is gone.

He's gone.

Day 98

Today my friend here gave me so much flack about not being available enough for her and too busy to spend time with her. She went on and on and her email deflated me like a pinprick to a balloon. By the time I finished explaining myself and subsequently feeling angry that I had to explain myself, I was too tired to write.

I want to write the story but her attack left me so bruised I barely want to lift my head.

What is wrong with people?

And what is wrong with me that they think it's ok to speak to me that way?

Now she's asked Brad and me to come for dinner and while a part of me wants to make peace and go, another part of me asks, why should I? Even dealing with this decision is bringing about an exhaustion that has dragged me down further.

What is wrong with people?

Do I end this friendship or is it worth salvaging? I have no gauge, no understanding, no explanation, and am not sure what to do.

Even thinking about that is exhausting.

I'm exhausted, and don't want to write anymore.

So, I won't.

Day 99

Today my day was spent with Marcella and Bill. It is the last time I'll see them here in Mexico for they leave on Saturday, and Brad is coming in on Friday.

Tomorrow I want a day just for me where I can relax and rest, but today was a wonderful day spent with wonderful friends.

They are a blessing to me, and I realize I need to be with people that uplift me, care about me, and encourage me. I need to be careful how much time I spend, if any, with the ones who bring me down.

I'm very fragile and breakable, and while I do want to die and leave this world, while I'm still here, I want no more pain.

My quota for pain has reached its limit, and if people can't be kind, I need to stop being so afraid to let them go.

My fear has destroyed my life, but now has attached itself like a comfortable friend. It is a friend I also need to learn to let go of.

Day 100

Today I want to hide under my bed and never come out.

Day 101

Today's topic will be appropriately titled, "Saints Amongst the Hairballs", as these words need to be immortalized and come from the wisdom of my friend, Dave.

I had emailed him last night and regaled him with stories of how I found this world to be incredibly cruel and wanted to hide under my bed, for I was very afraid of the people out there. I told him I felt very breakable and wondered if he felt breakable, too?

He responded by saying he was more afraid of what was under his bed, and that would be the last place he would choose to hide.

That comment made me laugh.

He then said that in his job he encountered many disagreeable people and the staff secretly called them "Hairballs"; you know, the things that get stuck in your throat you just can't quite clear out.

Just as he gets to the point in his day where he can't take any more hairballs, along comes a "saint" and totally makes his day. It could be a sweet little old lady needing help and thankful to receive, or just a customer with a good joke to tell. Whoever the saint may be, it gives my friend the little push he needs to continue to think humanity is not totally without redeeming qualities.

In conclusion, my friend Dave said, "Tonight I found myself once again searching around for one of those special people to redeem my faith in humanity. Needless to say, your email was a breath of fresh air."

That comment made me cry.

In my pain, I helped someone else; someone kind who also probably gives more than he's ever received.

Brad is flying in shortly and I need to get ready to go meet him.

Since I now have a terrible food fixation and eat when upset, nervous, excited or awake, I had made a breakfast that would delight any lumberjack and a few of his buddies. It was a meal of gargantuan proportions and I was stuffing down bite after bite.

Upon reading the email from Dave, my soul was soothed and the food was put aside. I had received kindness and wisdom from a kind and wise friend. I didn't need to medicate with food.

I am learning a lot about myself.

The only problem is it is too late to save my son.

Day 102 to 111

It's funny that when I'm with Brad, I feel no need to write my daily journal because I have a sense of comfort and safety.

This time I felt my emotions do a slight change and am wondering if I'm falling in love with him, or if it's just that I need somewhere to belong so desperately, I'm imagining myself falling in love with him. Somehow, though, this time he seemed better looking and wittier and wiser and all around more appealing, which made my heart-strings skip a beat and made me nervous for the first time since he and I have met.

I didn't like the feeling.

I didn't like feeling that vulnerable and opening up my heart to another human being because this human being is offering me only friendship in return. Sometimes he calls me his girlfriend, and my heart fills with fear, but when he backs away and says we are only friends, I seem to want him. Push, pull, pull, push; the age old game of who loves who and who will be the alpha male or female.

I know I don't have the energy to play the game and know I'm too afraid to play and lose, so probably will not play at all.

However, each time I'm with him, I grow closer and we have agreed we're family, just haven't figured out in what capacity.

Do I need him because I need someone to feel close to and feel comforted by, or do I need him for more?

I don't know.

Since he left two days ago, I, once again, feel lost and alone.

What did I do wrong?

What didn't I do right?

People worry about things all the time, but there fears never come to fruition. Mine do.

Also, since he's left I've been unable to sleep through the night. While he was here, I felt safe and slept many hours and was well rested.

I can't count on someone else to always be there to comfort me.

I wish I could.

This is too hard a journey to take alone.

And I feel very alone.

Day 112

Brad called me mercurial which means changeable, volatile, fickle and erratic. When he said that, I started singing "I'm just a mercurial girl", which is an offshoot of a Madonna song, "I'm just a material girl." He found my play on words amusing and I found his words true.

I don't really like being mercurial and yet admit now I am. Before, I was proud of the fact I was a woman who said what she meant and meant what she said. Now I struggle desperately to hold on to a fact and to do what I say I will do, for nothing has much meaning and details are just that; details. They are simply details without any rhyme or reason or any meaning.

I no longer care much for the details for what can matter now?

My friend, Heidi, and I haven't been getting along too well and I was surprised at my reaction. I was ready to let go of this budding friendship and yet had felt a kinship to her and thought we would be lifelong friends. Since I've been wrong about so much in my life, and realize now that I've never been a very good judge of character, I thought I'd just made another mistake in the choice of a friend.

Yet something still gnawed at me and I didn't want to give her up, so I asked her to come visit me today so we could talk. She agreed to come.

In talking I told her that while she thought I was ignoring her and laughing and having fun with other friends, there were many times she had hurt me and I had chosen to just keep quiet about it. Then, when she confronted me with her hurt, whether real or imagined, I felt it was unfair of her to do so.

I asked her who all these friends were that I was supposedly with and she thought I was with many people during my belly dancing classes and my walks on the beach.

When I told her I was alone during these times and really, she was my closest friend here in a friendless world, she seemed pacified.

Just speaking my thoughts and hurts also pacified me.

We needed to share and open up, something very difficult for me to do.

And right now, I can't take other peoples hurt feelings. I would rather be alone.

Truthfully, I would rather not be alone and have no hassles with anyone.

Heidi and I are now fine and I'm glad we cleared the air.

This is all just stuff, small stuff, unimportant stuff, stuff to make me plod one foot in front of the other.

It's all so unimportant and unnecessary and yet is part of the world I still live in.

God, take me out of this world.

Let me go.

Day 113

As I awake, the thoughts for what I'll be writing about are prevalent in my mind, but before I've even poured my morning coffee, my mood changes like the weather and I find myself writing about different subjects than originally planned.

The only constant is my deep ache for my son and my constant guilt at seeing how many places I failed him and was not there for him in his darkest hour.

For the hour must have been dark indeed to be able to put a gun to his head, or in his mouth, and pull the trigger, knowing he won't be able to change his mind; also knowing he doesn't know what's on the other side of death, but hurting too much to stop. Knowing that no matter what is waiting for him on the other side, this side has become so unbearable to exist in that he felt he had no other choice.

I know he would have explored every avenue to try and help himself, but just as I feel now, he must have felt so alone.

I was always so afraid that he felt as alone and unloved in this world as I've always felt but didn't want it to be true. I didn't want the person I loved the most to feel the same degree of anguish, despair and loneliness I was feeling.

He must have. In the end, he must have felt there was nowhere to turn, and in all honesty, I don't know where he could have turned to.

And the thought that he did feel even a semblance of what I've felt my entire life rips me apart.

I had a dream a few nights ago where two people had Kelly the dog pinned down and were causing her extreme pain. Her face was turned towards me and the pleading for help was almost palpable. She was pleading for me to help her and protect her, but I was too far away.

Frantically, I ran towards her, but it was almost as if I was running in slow motion, all the while watching these people cause her more and more pain. Her imploring eyes were fixed on mine as I struggled to close the distance between us, but it was taking forever and soon her eyes gave up hope and lost their grip on mine. "No", I screamed in my soundless voice! "No", I screamed in my defeat! "Don't give up!"

As the distance grew smaller and I was almost upon Kelly's captives, I hesitated, for I realized I didn't know what to do. I realized I didn't know how to help her. I felt helpless against these powerful foes. I couldn't save her.

I couldn't save her.

Of course, I understood Kelly the dog represented my son.

For my son and me, we were very similar. I only wanted us to be different because I felt I was so broken and a human beyond repair.

He loved me, and I loved him.

And now he's gone.

And I have no one to love.

And no one who loves me.

Many friends reading this will disagree and tell me to snap out of my vicious circle and cycle of self-pity. Many friends will tell me they love me and in a way, I suppose they do.

But this is my journal, my thoughts, my fears, my feelings, my heart, my soul.

And today all I feel is pain.

Day 114

I'm not too sure what to make of this day. I'm bored and restless and feel frustrated I don't have more friends to do things with. The few friends I've made are couples and while they include me in some things, they don't seem to include me in evening activities.

Evening activities is what I need. The days I can meander around and flitter away, but it's the nights I have a difficult time knowing what to do with myself. It's also the nights when I feel the most alone and the saddest.

Yesterday I went for lunch to Heidi's house and it was a very pleasant meal. She had other friends there too, and the topic of conversation was fairly light.

I struggled to keep abreast of what others were saying and found myself somehow trying to fill the time, the void, and the words just to make the day go by.

I'd told Heidi I needed to keep busy and sitting and visiting was very hard for me to do. Since she was hurt that I never came to her house, I went, but once again found the sitting and visiting hard to do. I squirmed in my chair, trying to find things to talk about, and the sheer effort of making polite talk exhausted me to the point where it became difficult to keep my eyes open and my thoughts clear.

I'm just not there people. My mind is fighting so hard to keep one step ahead of the grief completely engulfing me that I'm just not there.

Continually telling people this fact seems to fall on deaf ears for most want me to come over to sit and visit.

I don't know what to do because today I spent the day alone and it is too lonely. I don't like being this alone.

I think what I may want is someone there and present but not someone I need to entertain or make small talk with.

I guess I have that in my dog.

But, it's not enough...

Day 115

Today was quite a day, starting with the night. Before someone thinks I don't know the difference between day and night, let me explain. I hope I can do justice to this day without being restricted and restrained by my verbal inadequacies.

I had a dream; a dream where I went to visit a friend I didn't know in a house I didn't know and spent the night. Somewhere in the night I felt someone standing at the foot of my bed and recognized my friend, Curtis, from Florida. I don't know what he said but do know I asked him how he got in the house. He said he broke in and soon after left, without my knowing the reason for his visit.

Still in my dream, I woke my friend, told her about the visit and together we checked the doors to find they were easy to open and while this time a friend had visited me, maybe next time a foe would enter in.

We both became afraid.

I woke up and questioned the significance of such a dream.

I was still afraid.

Throughout the day I had a sense my son was trying to visit but my fear holds him back.

I am very afraid.

For if I see him, I will want to go to be with him.

I will want to go more than I want to go now.

So I sense he is watching over me and trying to protect me, but it should have been I who protected him.

It is wrong that, even now, my son still tries to look after me.

I didn't do a good enough job of looking after him.

Later that morning I checked for my daily email from Brad, for it is one constant in my life. In his email today he said he only felt towards me as a sister and hoped we could just be friends.

Deep inside I knew this was who we were and knew I was not emotionally at a place where I could have a love relationship but I only saw it as further rejection.

I saw it only as someone else not being able to love me.

I saw it as further proof I am to be alone and unloved.

I saw it as losing someone I cared about again.

It was too much.

Thankfully I held back any sharp retorts and told him to give me some time. I told him I was upset and this was not a conversation that should have happened by email. What I wanted to say was that for a man who only wanted to be friends, he sure came to Mexico a lot, and he persistently invited me to Arizona. Maybe he was looking for the girl he had met the year before, whose son was still alive. Maybe he was looking for the girl who was fun and funny and witty and personable and a good friend. Maybe I was looking for her, too, all the while knowing she had died with her son.

We can't change the past, but what I did see in my present is that Brad was very vocal whenever he was dissatisfied with something not going his way, while I kept silent. It was easier to keep silent. I want someone to understand how incredibly difficult it is for a person in grief to stand up for themselves. We are so defeated by the tragedy to end all tragedies that taking on more grief or strife is inconceivable.

It just reminded me of all the times before when I cared and no one cared back.

And yet I wonder if there were some who cared for me and I never cared back.

Did I bring all this about?

Did my fears bring about my consequences?

Then please let me die, God, for I am full of fear.

I have had the most horrible consequences possible and still there is no reprieve.

I truly don't want to struggle and fight and try again.

Getting the email from Brad sent me into a state of shock. It was further shock upon shock and I sensed my entire being trying to close up inside. I sensed a defeated attitude and one where I could only fail.

I don't know how else to be when confronted with rejection, whether real or imagined.

I run.

I hide.

I'm afraid.

I know Brad would continue to be my friend but I don't know if I can be.

I let myself care again, knowing it was the wrong thing to do.

I knew he was a man who would only be a friend.

But I let myself fall anyway.

I feel to end the chapter here, but there is something more I need to say.

The rest of the day I felt as if I was being led. I felt I was part of a much bigger picture.

While I wanted to run and hide, I knew there was something or someone watching over me this day.

Kelly the dog and I wandered aimlessly and soon found ourselves walking the beach in Guayabitos. Couple after couple passed us and it made me feel all the more alone. I wondered why I can't just resign myself to the fact I am to be alone, and accept it. I can't. I can't. I can't. It seems to be such a waste of a warm, loving person, for inside I know that is who I am.

But I was also a mother who loved her child and yet failed him.

How can I bear this world with him gone?

Did all my fears bring this about?

Further walking the beach I spotted two different individuals I knew and asked both if they would like to go to happy hour at a hotel. Both said no, but something propelled me further and I knew I was to go.

Kelly the dog and I arrived at the hotel and seated ourselves quietly by the pool. Within minutes two women started talking to me for one had recognized Kelly the dog. I opened up and told them the man I cared about just broke up with me by email. I also told them I had just lost my son. It was all too much for me to bear.

I saw they were both very uncomfortable with hearing my tale of woe and wanted to be on their way to drink their beers and laugh the day away. One lady left quickly while the other stayed for a few moments. She said everything has a reason and I may one day be happy this man wasn't the one. One day I might look at today and think this was a good thing. She also said she believed in karma and that we get what we deserve.

I must have really pissed karma off...

Day 116

Why don't I want to write today? Why have I procrastinated all day, basically whittling and flittering away the day, and have only started to write in the evening?

There is a lot to write about. There are many hurts and foibles and picturesque scenes to write about. Why don't I want to write? Because I'm not talking to Brad.

He's emailed twice. I haven't read the emails and am afraid.

Fear seems to motivate everything I do, think or feel now.

Maybe it always has.

Maybe it's become my best friend.

It is a terrible friend to have and only takes; takes away your peace of mind, takes away your rationalizing abilities, takes away your other friends, takes away your loved ones, takes away your self-respect, takes away your capacity to function.

I've always feared love.

I've feared loving and never being loved in return.

For the most part, my fears have been realized.

Now I walk in fear that my fears are all I have that remain constant.

I was afraid, after the horrendous childhood my son had, that he would not outlive me.

My fear was realized.

People say we bring about what we fear.

In that case, did I bring about his death?

Did I fear it so much I made it happen?

Now I fear losing my mind and being alone.

I don't know which is worse for if I lose my mind, I

won't know any different and whatever happens to me will happen.

I guess I fear being alone more.

Now that I am so consumed with this fear of being alone, I search for rejection around every corner. I search for it to come about, because when it does, I can stop fearing.

Like my child dying.

Now, I no longer have to fear that he will...

Day 117

Last night my new friend, Jean, and I went to hear Mexican entertainment in the park and, in a different time, in a different world, it would have been fabulous. There were street dancers costumed in vivid colors with bright feathers in their hair. There was a Mariachi band and fireworks and for the most part, people were jovial and in a happy mood.

To me, it was simply more hours I was filling and a means to an end. After it was over, I would go home to bed and another day would be done.

It would be another day closer to the day of my death.

That is what I focus on now and that is what I want, all the while knowing what I really want is for my son to be alive, and for him and me to be living happy, fruitful lives.

If he couldn't make it, then neither can I.

If he couldn't find a reason to go on, neither can I.

He was a part of me and I was a part of him.

People tell me I need to find a reason to go on, but I don't want to. That is the problem with my grief. I want to give up. I want to give in to it. I want the days to end.

That's not what I really want.

I want to live a happy and prosperous life knowing all is well with my son.

Hoping the night air and late night would exhaust me I still took my daily allowance of sleeping pills and quickly fell asleep. Three a.m. found me awake, afraid and alone and that was it for the night.

It hit me how alone I really am, and how much I lean on friends like Brad. I think I lean so much they fall over. While I know that and try hard to show myself to be an independent woman, I still need someone to be there, especially at this time. It is terrifying to me when no one is there to comfort me, for I need to feel loving arms around me and hear words of compassion and caring.

It appears to be that, in life, I love more than I am loved. It appears to be that, in life, people can give me up quicker than I can give them up. It appears to be that, in life, I lose more than I win.

I just wish it was a heritage I didn't pass on to my son for he had so many wonderful gifts. He had so many reasons to live a full and rich life. He was beaten down and beaten down, but deserved so much more.

Yesterday, while at the concert, I took Kelly the dog for a pee. We wandered towards the ocean and I stood and watched the ocean waves approach and recede in the dark. It was a peaceful, calming moment and I cherish and crave those more and more.

As we turned to go back, two couples came out of the restaurant to our right. Kelly and I quickly maneuvered to miss bumping into them and were successful in our endeavor. One of the ladies hadn't noticed us and when she quickly turned and saw Kelly, let out an expletive of "F...ing dog."

Her words cut me to the core and produced a pain deep inside. Instantly I felt protective and whereas before, would have said nothing, this time asked her what she said. She mumbled, "Nothing" and we all continued on our way, but it made me think of so many times people were cruel to my son and I said nothing.

I defended my dog, because now I have nothing to lose.

Why didn't I defend my son?

He might still be here.

Day 118

Today I feel under the weather. My throat is sore, my skin is clammy and my chest feels as though an elephant is sitting on it. Instantly a black mood becomes blacker, a sad day becomes sadder, a mad moment becomes madder.

I somehow feel I'd reached my quota of kaka in my life and that now, after experiencing the worst pain possible, would be free from all encumbrances. I would now be free to just live and grieve and wish daily to die.

It is not to be.

I still have to deal with normal life circumstances, with normal people having pissy days and with more loss, more pain, more sickness, more sadness, and more grief.

Have I not paid the ultimate price to this unforgiving world when it took my son?

Have I not proved I can take a licking and keep on ticking?

Apparently not.

I feel so alone.

It's not anyone's responsibility to make me feel less alone but I truly feel so alone.

I am mixed up inside, my emotions are all askew, I appear to function rationally and yet I am a mess.

No wonder no one wants to be around.

No wonder I can't find love in this loveless world.

People tell me to speak affirmations and I want to shove those affirmations down their throat.

Don't they know all I've ever done is look for the positive and wait for a good outcome?

Also, apparently not.

Sickness makes one sad; sadness makes one sadder.

I think I'll go to bed.

Day 119

I am very sick today. It would appear the lung infection is back so I went to the doctor. He agreed with my prognosis and I am now on antibiotics and a myriad of other get well products.

Spending the day in bed leaves me too much time to think. Too much time to think leaves me sadder than sad.

It is a conundrum with no end.

Back to bed I go.

Day 120

Still sick today and had a sleepless, restless, clammy, sweat filled night. Am trying to be wiser than last time I got this sick and am staying in bed, although I want nothing more than to go outside.

My neighbors, Val and Betty, have been taking Kelly the dog out for her pee and are very gracious and kind.

Why do I have such a hard time accepting when people are gracious and kind?

Why don't I feel I deserve it?

I need to just relax and be.

I want to write more positive things in this daily journal and yet feel that would not be true to self. I don't feel positive and somehow need to write my true feelings and true thoughts.

Some days I think it is time to end this book or journal, but then I continue on. I continue on because I need to believe that someday this will be a book and will help some other mother going through what I'm going through. Right now this journal is all that is giving me a purpose of any sort, albeit a small one.

If I find I've only been writing this for me and it really is of no use to anyone else, I will feel shattered and more broken than before.

Somewhere, somehow my life has to have some meaning.

Everything I have attempted to do I have failed at. Now I am attempting to write a book in hopes of immortalizing my son and yet still pouring out my feelings.

Some days I feel I fail miserably at trying to convey my thoughts on paper, but some days I feel I succeed.

It is those days I succeed I am hanging on to.
I need to go to bed.
I am sick.

Day 121

I am still sick today; sick and very weak in body and mind. Lying in bed, not having energy to do much of anything gives me too much time to think, and all I think about is my son.

Wherever I venture, in my mind, I only see where I've failed him. I only see how I tried the best I knew how, but it wasn't good enough, and we failed.

Today I cried out to God and begged him to take me. I told him I was tired of life, tired of living, and to please be merciful and take me from this world.

What I seemed to hear in my mind was, "Not yet."

Day 122

I am still sick and in bed, and have now lost count as to how many days it has been. While I'm sure, in actuality, it has only been a few days, to me, it seems like a lifetime.

Frantically hitting the channel changer, repeatedly going round and round the channels in a desperate attempt to find some program that will take my mind off what's on my mind for a mere pittance, I toss it aside and grab ahold of whatever medication is available to ease the pain, both external and internal; both in my body and in my soul.

Nothing salves.

Nothing soothes.

Nothing makes me feel better.

Nothing makes this life worthwhile.

I now see this world as hateful and cruel. I now see this world as one I no longer want to exist in. I now see this world as a world that took my son.

The neighbors knock on the door with a smoothie to coat my throat and a commitment to walk Kelly the dog while I'm ill.

I cry when I see people in this world who are kind.

My neighbors are kind.

Day 123

I'm hiding from the world. It is convenient my body decided to become ill just about the time my soul became afraid to venture out.

I was saddened by Brad's rejection, all the while knowing it was the right thing and that, romantically, we are wrong together. It still hurts.

Now I'm doing what I always do and don't know how to stop. I'm avoiding him, avoiding emailing him and slightly worried at how I'll feel when he comes back to this part of Mexico in three weeks.

He will be bringing his daughter and her friend and for all intents and purposes, this is not a visit to see me, although, of course we will see each other. I am afraid of my unruly emotions and no longer know how to curtail them. What if I do find them running amok with a will of their own?

I don't know how to go back to just being friends.

As his email blindsided me and caused me to back away in shock, I've now braced myself for the time when he will tell me he's met someone. While I know he will still be my friend, our dynamics will change and his attention will be on his new love.

That idea terrifies me for right now, I need him. I need him so badly as to imagine myself in love with him.

This is a man who calms me, a man who holds me while I sleep, and a man who is always there for me. Of course, I would think I'm in love. I would probably give him a kidney or anything else he may need, just for the fact that I feel safe enough to sleep when he is around.

For when he is not around I take the maximum allotted sleeping pills and still can't sleep. I try and nap during the day and cannot. I feel tired and listless and irritable and lethargic all day.

When he is around, I sleep hours and hours and actually laugh throughout the day. While my grief is paramount and will never leave, being with Brad gives me moments of reprieve.

No wonder I don't want someone else to have him.

This is not rocket science...

Day 124

I have so much to say today, and yet am so tired. I'm tired. My body is tired, my mind is tired, my soul is tired, my spirit is tired.

I told God again today how tired I am, and asked Him to take me.

The tears I'd been holding back the last few days finally let loose last night and I didn't find them healing. I only found them more tiring, for no matter how much I cry, I feel no better.

My son is still gone.

I'm tired, God. I'm tired, God.

Please release me from this life.

I spent another restless day in bed, the only visitors being the wonderful neighbors to see if Kelly or I needed anything. I needed little, Kelly needed to pee. The knocks on my door were welcome for it gave me a sense of belonging in a world I feel alien to.

There was a knock on my door I didn't hear today because I was sleeping. When I awoke, a man I'd met some weeks ago had called and left a note hoping I would feel better soon.

It is evident he is interested.

It makes me sad.

For mere interest means little to me and I no longer have any hope to be loved. There has always been interest in me and yet I've spent most of my life alone.

I will not entertain the prospect of this man, nor will I even say his name, for he will not be part of this story.

I also realize I am writing about nonsensical things because what I want to write about is too painful for me. I am holding back the floodgates that are bursting to come out. I am holding back writing about my deep sorrow, my deep pain, the places I failed my son, the places this world failed him, his deep sorrow, his deep pain.

I can't. I can't. I can't.

I must.

Day 125

I feel delirious. I feel sweaty and clammy and bored and sad and lonely and like my brain cells are not connecting to each other.

I miss my son.

I feel sorry for him.

I feel sorry for myself.

I feel so sorry for myself that I don't fault anyone for not hitching up to this wagon.

I'm going to quit writing.

I'm on a downward spiral.

Day 126

I don't want to write today. I don't want to write today because I don't feel I can do justice to the day. I don't feel I can find all the necessary words to explain what is happening to me. I don't feel I can find the necessary words to describe how deep my pain is and how unfathomable it is for me to face it.

For I've been running. I've been running away from the pain. I don't fault myself for running for what good would facing it do? What good would facing the inexorable, unyielding, unalterable grief I feel be?

What would it accomplish for me to face my darkest hour?

What would it accomplish for me to accept the death of my son?

As long as I can keep running, running, running, hiding, hiding, hiding, at least I can take a breath.

When the enormity of what has happened tries to slide its way into the recesses of my mind, I can't breathe. I can't find any purpose for being.

I don't want to find a purpose for being, all the while continuing to write. For it is in writing, that I feel there might be some vague reason for my being. It is in writing, that I feel I can somehow chronicle the painful details that were my son's and my life.

Yet the words hold me back. The constant threat of tears holds me back. The unimaginable pain of facing that he's gone holds me back.

Even now I want to run.

I want to quit writing and I want to run.

Escape. Escape. Escape.

Where will I flee to?

There is nowhere to go that still has my son.

Except for Heaven...

Then to Heaven I want to go.

Is it even a real place?

Or is it someplace we made up because the longing for our departed loved ones would be too excruciating to bear if we had no hope to ever see them again?

Once again, this was not what I'd intended to write.

Once again, this was what needed to be said.

Day 127

I lost my camera. Left it behind in a restaurant last week and today, when I went back to see if by any slim chance it was still there, the waiter didn't even get up from the table to go check.

It was gone.

And it's just another thing weighing me down.

I can't take even the smallest thing going wrong.

And yet, one thing after another goes wrong.

And yes, it's my own fault I lost the camera. I should have paid more attention.

I'm just in a funk.

And I do realize I'm thinking too much about Brad and feeling he got off the hook too easy. My thoughts may be all irrational, but it feels as though everyone can toss me aside, treat me how they want, and I forgive and forget.

Except I no longer forgive and forget.

Now, everything bugs me and everyone bugs me.

And I don't see this world as friendly at all.

I need to stop writing.

I feel so much emotion and thoughts and feelings inside, but they are a jumble, all in a tumble in my mind, and when I open my mouth to speak, or sit at my computer to type, it is so painful, so incredibly painful, to face the loss I'm having to live with, that I toss the words in the air and care not where they land. I let the sentences collide into themselves and say nothing while saying meaningless, endless, trivial words.

It is plodding one foot in front of the other.

What am I continuing for?

What matters a camera or a potential lost love?

What matters any of it?

It is merely something else for me to focus on in trying to escape my grief.

If only for a brief moment before it rushes back into my soul.

Today I danced on the street.

It was the Mexican Mardi Gras here in La Penita.

While I danced on the street with a nameless Mexican man, I forgot.

For a brief moment, I forgot.

Then the music stopped and I remembered.

I can't keep dancing forever.

Day 128

I would wonder if all grieving parents instantly become ADD or if it's just me and the few I know? While I've noticed the similarity of coping methods in other grieving parents, I've learnt I can only speak for myself and am only responsible for my own thoughts and emotions.

It would appear that since our world has been thrown into utter and complete darkness, we are as the blind, stumbling and groping along, hoping to find our way, but unable to see any of it clearly.

For I've said many times before, what does anything matter now? What does it matter what I wear, what I feel, what I do, or what I speak?

And so many times I find my mouth opening, the words escaping and careening helter skelter, landing where they may. I endeavor to never say cruel words and would hope I've succeeded in my quest. What I find more so, is the words make little sense.

I want someone to crawl into this gargantuan vacuum left by my son's passing which I used to call my soul. I want someone to fully understand the enormity of what I am living with and living in. I want someone to be as a second skin to me for I feel so very alone and so very afraid to face what I'm facing; a life without my son; a world without him in it.

I function on automatic pilot and need everything to remain the same in a world where nothing will ever again be the same. I want a small corner of my life to make sense in a world that will never make sense again. I want to feel I am not running so fast as to try and outrun the grief.

I want to say what is truly in my heart but I can't bear the words that are just sitting there, smoldering, waiting to erupt, wanting to be said. I can't bear to tap into the reservoir of the unsaid words that would sufficiently explain the magnitude of what I'm feeling. I can't bear it, so like a hamster on a wheel, I go round and round and round, faster and faster, running from the words, running from the feeling.

I see other mothers, whose loss has been longer than mine, do the same.

They bounce here, they jump there, they grab onto anyone offering a helping hand that may pull them out of the muck and mire that has become their existence.

Is this what awaits me?

If I let go of the bottled up grief, will I appear, for all intents and purposes, to act as though I've lost my mind?

For, in some parallel universe way we grieving parents have lost our minds. We can't cope or understand or find any significance to our loss and so our minds are scrambling trying to make sense out of the minutest of details.

That is why we can't bear to have anything more change. I need to prepare my coffee the night before and panic if I haven't. I need to have my toothbrush and toothpaste, along with face creams, in the same spot and panic if they aren't. I need to know everything is fine between you and me, whoever you may be, because I panic if I have to deal with anyone else's trauma or drama.

I am hanging on by my fingertips and could lose hold at any second and fall, fall, fall into the bottomless pit of despair.

I understand how homeless people lose their will to better themselves.

I understand how alcoholics lose themselves in their bottle trying to ease the pain.

I understand how drug addicts want that next hit just to erase the memory of whatever their grief may be.

I understand how someone could lose their mind and exist in a semi living state with the body alive but the mind already dead.

I understand how someone could push away anyone who would even try to love them as they would be so afraid that person would die.

I understand how you could close up inside so completely as to never feel again.

I understand.

I just don't want to become one of them...

Day 129

Today was interspersed with happy and sad. Betty and Val, who live next door to me, had invited me for breakfast and I accepted without knowing what to do with Kelly the dog, as they were my principle dog sitters.

Knocking on David and Jean's door, my other neighbors in this complex, brought no answer to my knock, so I knew whatever I was to do this day, I was to do it with Kelly.

Today is a Thursday and Thursday is always market day in La Penita, full of Mexicans selling their wares hoping to entice the touristas (tourists) to buy something they couldn't live without. Walking by the market dwellers, their common chant to any passersby is to come in and buy something you don't need. It causes you to chuckle and sometimes the very audacity of that statement causes people to buy something they don't need, all the while positive they do.

Walking towards the market, Kelly the dog in tow, and wondering if I would find Betty and Val to tell them I couldn't come, I see David and Jean and they kindly take Kelly off my hands. I was able to meet for breakfast and walk the market, unencumbered by my trusty perro.

Funny how things work out, isn't it?

I used to be a bit of a believer that things just work how they're supposed to.

Now, I no longer believe that.

How could I, for that would mean my son was meant to go?

I no longer know what I believe and that is a frightening place to be, for we all need some vision, some purpose, some hope, some as yet undiscovered conquest to conquer.

When you lose all that, you truly don't know how to be.

I don't know how to be.

I struggle for conversation and meet people I have no recollection of meeting when I supposedly see them a second time. They approach me and are confident in the retelling of our last conversation, while I endeavor to remember ever having met them. The simple fact they know my name and know minimal facts about me would cause me to believe them.

No one makes an impression any more.

The one who made the biggest impression on my life is gone.

Who else matters?

Let me clarify.

Who else matters to me?

Day 130

Today was a sad day where I could not find a place for myself, so kept myself inside my apartment. Last night I allowed myself to feel some of the deep, buried pain and cried long into the night. The tears don't help; they just make me see the senselessness of crying them.

For what could it change? And what could improve now that my child is gone?

Tomorrow was to have been the memorial for my son that the Russian culture observes in order to honor the deceased. It is to happen before the day of their passing and makes me realize that, one year ago, my son was still alive.

In two weeks the date will be March 25th, one year exactly to the day I heard my son was dead.

I cancelled the memorial to remember him and opted to stay in Mexico instead.

Now, I question the wisdom of my decision as maybe some comfort from friends would make this day a little less unbearable.

The small family I do have didn't acknowledge the day at all, and I wonder at how easy it seems for people to forget my son and I. I truly do feel we were throwaway people, and if anyone does care, this would be the time to tell me.

It is too painful to continue to write. I am afraid for tomorrow, for somehow Kelly the dog and I will attempt to have this memorial, just the two of us.

It will truly show how alone I am.

I hope I'm wrong.

I understand how my son must have felt.

Without hope...
Without love...
Without joy...
Only pain...

Day 131

Today was a very sad day. As mentioned earlier, Russian tradition has a memorial that is to occur before the one year mark of their passing and today would have been the day I was to have the service if I went back home.

As I'd decided to cancel my ticket home and stay in Mexico longer, I thought today would be commemorated with just Kelly and me doing a service of sorts.

To the best of my understanding, the soul still hovers above us until this service occurs and then it is free to go to its final resting place. If I'm wrong, I stand corrected, but as best as I can fathom, this was to be a day where I was to say an even more final goodbye to my son.

How many goodbyes can I say?

I've yet to grasp ahold of the fact he is even gone.

In the past few days I'd questioned my decision to forego the ritual back home and stay behind here to do the best I could.

Today I questioned it even more for I felt a sense of loss I've yet to feel. It is clear to me I am beginning to truly grieve, for I know that until now, I have been holding it in.

It was, and is, just too painful to bear.

And I question how this could be done in a proper way for no matter what, my son is still gone.

Restless and agitated, I slept fitfully only to awaken in the early afternoon. Somewhere through the night I'd taken Kelly the dog into my bed and she snored peacefully beside me. It gave me comfort of sorts, but was not enough.

Today I needed to honor my son.

Leaving the apartment, I realized I did not want to face this day alone with Kelly the dog. I wanted someone beside me to care while I cried.

As Kelly and I walked down our street, I looked behind me and there was my neighbor, Jan. Approaching her, with tears streaming down my face, I told her what today was and said I couldn't do this alone. I asked that she please come with me and she quickly agreed.

This is a kind person.

I have met kind people here in Mexico and realize it is me who has changed to where I now have difficulty recognizing them.

Jan, Kelly and I proceeded to the flower shop where I bought thirty three large white daisies, one for every year my son was alive. I didn't know how I was going to do this service, but knew it would unfold as it may.

Jan didn't want to cross the suspension bridge over to Guayabitos and we agreed to meet on the rock bluffs in between. Kelly and I walked the distance and climbed the rocks to where we were the only ones sitting atop the rock bluffs, the ocean waves below.

The tears flowed. The sadness in my heart surfaced and would not be held back. I cried and I cried and realized I was finally truly grieving. Hiding from the grief did not lesson the pain and while I don't understand what purpose the tears are, I know they have to come.

Kelly stood beside me as I tossed the flowers into the ocean, sometimes missing the water and having them land in the rocks below. The flowers that did make it into the ocean swayed with the waves and I watched as they went further and further from the shore.

I cried.

Then, I cried some more.

Jan arrived with helium balloons and one by one, we let them go to the ozone. I watched the balloons until I could see them no more and wondered if my son was there to witness this sight.

As thirty three large daisies were surrounded by the ocean water, I watched them bounce and weave on the water's edge. It was a moment of peace. I prayed for my son. I spoke to my son.

I can't do justice to this day.

Words fail me.

If Russian tradition is correct, I just released him to go to his final resting place.

It was too hard to do.

I wanted him to stay and watch over me.

Day 132

How sad I am for my little boy. How sad I am for the life he lived and the way he died. How sad I am that somehow the cruelty of events in his life wore him down to where he couldn't see any other way.

It would seem to me, since I've taken a step back from my attachment to Brad, and he to me, that I am now feeling the emotions I should have always felt and dealt with, but instead tried to hide behind him. I tried to pretend at least half of me was a normal woman with a normal life and I pushed the grieving process to the side.

Now it won't be pushed aside anymore and has come to the forefront of my life. I need to grieve my son, but what a horrendous undertaking it is. Even before, in a world where he still lived, I thought a parent losing a child was unthinkable and my heart hurt for nameless, faceless people experiencing this incredible pain.

Little did I know I would someday be one of them.

My heart hurts so much for my child that I feel all energy receding from my body and conversation is an effort. I hear my neighbors talking outside on the rooftop and any desire to join them is quickly taken over by my exhaustion.

Am I sick physically?

I may be.

Am I sick emotionally?

I may be.

Am I sick with grief?

I am.

I'm too tired, so will go and lay down.

I'm ready to leave Mexico.

I just don't know where to go.

Day 133

I am ready to leave here. Yes, the days are warm and sunny, but the weather never did make or break my mood so matters little in my thoughts for the day.

I've walked the beach in Guayabitos with my loyal perro beside me and repeatedly thrown the stick into the water for her to chase. While it still makes passersby stop, stare and smile, it now brings me no amusement and has become more of a chore.

I've struggled along in my limited Spanish, and whereas before I saw it as a challenge to be understood, now I rarely bother and choose to say nothing instead.

I endeavored to make friends here and while I've made a few I'm thankful for, they will go their way and I will go mine. The person I was last year in Arizona, who made lifelong friends in a millisecond, is no longer me.

My sleepless state has left me irritable and annoyed, if at no one else but myself. I take whatever pill I can get my hands on when three a.m. turns into four; four a.m. turns into five; five a.m. turns into six, and I am still lying there, awake and in the deepest sorrow known to man.

It is a bad time of day to grieve.

Any time is a bad time of day to grieve.

It brings you no respite; it brings you no calm.

Like a tidal wave, it gains more momentum and grows larger every day.

I've tried to run from this grief these past months and now am even embarrassed and ashamed at how I tried to pretend everything was as it was before. I tried to pretend everything was normal in a world that will never be normal again. I tried to make jokes, have fun, fall in love, be who I used to be, but I will never be her again.

Don't tell me I will become someone better.

How can I when my child found no reason to live?

I am the mother.

My job was to protect him when he was little and steer him on a safe course when he was grown.

I failed at my job and created a young man who couldn't fail.

Not even at death...

Yes, I am ready to leave here.

I just am not ready to go home.

Day 134

It is late in the evening as I'm sitting down to write, and I'm tired. Why did I wait so long to write as I know mornings are best?

Sometimes I can't find words to say what I want to say. And sometimes I feel like this is a journal with perpetual whining and in describing myself, I'm describing a person who doesn't want to try anymore.

I'm describing someone without hope, without direction, and without a purpose or a cause. The small glimpse of anything worthwhile left for me to do is maybe writing this book, so then I second guess what I say, what I feel and what I type, and figure it should somehow be more entertaining.

More entertaining?

Have I lost my senses?

It is a book about a mother grieving her only child.

And I want to be more entertaining?

What is wrong with me?

Better yet, what is right with me?

Many would say I have a multitude of redeeming qualities, my strength of character being one of them. Since I've attained adulthood many years ago, many have said I am the strongest woman they know or have ever met.

I never understood whether I was supposed to feel gratified or flattered when people thought I was strong, and used to say I didn't want to be strong. I wanted to live a life where my greatest problem was my pantyhose ripping and that fact alone would cause me to quiver and shiver in distress and an inability to cope with anything more.

For I believed if I could not cope with anything more grievous than my pantyhose ripping, then the world or the universe or God would not give me anything more to deal with. In my life, that was not to be, so then I took on another belief.

I believed that as I climbed one hurdle and didn't lose my sanity, lose my belief in God, lose my hope, lose my trust in mankind, that I would then have to just climb another hurdle. I only hoped and prayed God would be merciful to me and let the anguish that was my life, subside.

It was not to be.

And my greatest fear was that my son would not outlive me.

It was a fear that ate away at me night and day.

I only hoped and prayed it would be a fear that would not be realized.

What is worth writing about now?

Day 135

I dream of my son. At night, in my sleep, I dream of him, and I am happy. I visit with him and we live the life we were meant to live; one full of family that loves us, friends that laugh with us, a life of contentment and joy.

Then, I awake.

And I ache.

I ache with sorrow. And I plod along.

I feel tired in my heart today, feel tired in my soul, feel the weariness permeate my very being and don't know what else to say.

So, I will say nothing more...

Day 136

Could I be having a nervous breakdown? I've never had a nervous breakdown before, so have no way of knowing, but feel as if I'm floating somewhere between this world and beyond. Everything pales in significance down here on earth and when I look up to the sky, wonder if my son can see me.

I wonder if he can reach down to me, but am so limited and held down by this world that I can't reach up to him?

And I wonder how I come up with questions like these?

I don't remember questioning these queries before.

But then, I don't remember much of anything anymore.

I can't even remember if I've written, in the past few chapters, that my credit card was compromised here in Mexico, and now I have no way to get any money to live on down here.

I panicked and felt suspended in time, lightheaded and dizzy from the fear, for now my safety net is gone. I don't know who my safety net is anymore and while friends have since helped me, I panicked first and asked questions later.

Who was my son's safety net?

Where could he turn to when he panicked financially or any other way?

The only one he could turn to was me, but where was I?

Rarely in a place where I could help him.

I ache for him.

I can't bear not to talk to him.

I ache for him.

He was my son.

It should have been me and not him.

I ache for my son and now have more and more difficulty sleeping.

Last night the thoughts about my son wouldn't leave me be and let me sleep, so I ingested pill after pill hoping for some solace to alleviate my despair. I didn't care if I didn't wake up today; I never care to wake up the next day. What I cared about was the anguish of my soul dissipating long enough for me to fall asleep.

I'm always disappointed when I awaken.

Today I went to Western Union here in La Penita and awaited funds from my friend back home. It would help me to survive down here and I will have to ask more friends for it won't be enough.

The nice thing is I do have friends to ask, and also friends who will help me in my dire straits.

In the evening I got together with everyone else living in this complex and we played cards. I love playing cards and while I don't forget, I can put my grief to the side, if just for a moment.

One of the ladies started talking about grandchildren, something I'll now never have, and I became agitated and distraught. Not wanting them to know the turmoil I was feeling inside, I hurriedly progressed the card game along so everyone would have to concentrate and not have time to finish their conversation. My ploy didn't work and I felt I would start screaming when thankfully, they finished talking grandchildren and moved on to another topic, no one the wiser.

It's always there, isn't it?

It's always going to be there in my life.

The grief, I mean.

The knowing my child is gone will always be there.

There is no escape.

The best I can hope for in this hopeless world is a few moments of enjoyment.

I can never hope for more.

Day 137

Today was a tiring day. Kelly and I walked the beach to the end of Guayabitos and I threw the stick in the ocean for her on more than one occasion. She rushed into the waves, her main focus on the stick bobbing in the water, mindless of the large ocean waves.

A few times as she had the stick grasped firmly in her mouth, intent on reaching the shore, a colossal wave would rise up and overpower her making her, for the moment, invisible to the eye. My breath would catch and I'd rush into the water hoping to save my perro from any danger, knowing she was too far away for me to reach if a wave did sweep her out to sea; also knowing I was the one who threw the stick so far away as to put her in some danger.

She always persevered and swam towards shore, stick in mouth, and waited for more.

My perro is a survivor and a good dog.

I love her, just hate the reason I have her.

Walking back from Guayabitos midafternoon, we spotted the beginnings of a parade preparing to march towards the avenida. With my limited Spanish, I enquired as to when this parade was to start and was told in ten minutes.

Kelly and I were hungry, tired, had no water left and the camera a friend had lent me was still sitting in my apartment. Rushing as on fire, I quickly grabbed the camera, made a sandwich, threw some water in my bag and we ran back to the avenida to await the parade.

And wait we did.

When will I learn I'm in Mexico where nothing is a rush? No one is in a hurry and ten minutes could mean anything from an hour to a year.

My perro and I sat in the avenida eating our sandwich, drinking our water and waited.

What else was there to do?

We then walked to the beach in La Penita and watched the sunset which, once again, did nothing to enthrall. The sun went down. The end.

It's lonely in La Penita.

It's lonely in this world.

I miss my son.

He was my place of belonging.

Now I have none.

Day 138

People need to be gentler with us grieving parents. Well, actually no one owes us anything; it is just a hope of mine, for we are so wounded, so fragile, so breakable that we may shatter into a thousand pieces if even the slightest thing goes wrong.

Our hearts and souls are already shattered. All that is holding us together is the sinew of our body and the meagre struggles in our mind. Sometimes it feels as though I am desperately grasping ahold of sanity, for there is a fear my mind no longer wants to struggle to survive.

My son used to say, "Mom, if someone goes crazy, how do they know? They're crazy." Those and countless other witty comments he used to make caused me hours of amusement and I was known to quote my wise son many times.

He was wise. He had many attributes. The world is a sadder place without his wisdom, insight and humor. The sad thing is the world doesn't even know what it missed.

Today is a sad day.

I don't want to write anymore...

Day 139

Today I need to be alone.
Today I need to be with people.
Today I need to be alone with people.
I am in the perfect place in La Penita.
I can be alone in the midst of a crowd.
I am so tired I can barely sit and type.

Yesterday, I went out for dinner with my neighbors, Val and Betty, and their friends. Making polite conversation grew so exhausting for me that I felt tired, agitated, and while I didn't want to be alone, I didn't want to be with people either.

What am I to do?

After we came home, Val sat with me for a while and I told her how difficult it was for me to function throughout a day. I also told her this Friday would be a year since I heard my son had passed; a year with no direction, a year with no purpose, a year with no future, a year with no past. It was a year and it passed in a blink of an eye.

How many more will I have to endure?

Val wanted me to open up and talk about my son, and I wanted to push her away. The thought of opening my heart up, even a little, caused me distress I had difficulty concealing. I wanted her to stop trying to help because there is no help to be had.

Somehow I need to work through this on my own.

I would rather not.

I would rather not do the legwork needed to lead even a reasonable facsimile of a normal life.

I would just rather not.

I would rather give up.

I am tired.

This is not what I meant to say today. There is so much more to say.

I'm just so tired.

Day 140

Today is the one year anniversary of the official day my son died. His death certificate reads March 21, 2010, one year from today.

In what universe is it comprehensible that a mother would write the words "death certificate" about her son?

Day 141

Yesterday Kelly the dog and I walked the beach to Guayabitos and then stood and watched the ocean waves for a very long time. I walked partway into the water and let the warm waves gently slap against my legs and felt almost mesmerized by the rush of the ocean water.

Kelly the dog stood some distance away on the shore and when I would look behind me, her gaze never wavered from mine. I wonder what she was thinking.

I think I love this dog too much.

I have so much bottled up love inside and now, nowhere to give it to or maybe there is somewhere to give my love to, but I am too afraid.

It is too painful when that love is abruptly stopped and you're left teetering, floundering, wondering what to do knowing the person you care about the most is no longer there.

Walking home, I wished I had someone who knew and cared about my son to share part of this day with me. I felt sad that Kelly and I were so alone and so far away, although wasn't sure how being back in Canada would make it any better.

There are no words for anyone to say.

As I climbed the stairs to my apartment and rounded the hallway towards my door, there was a beautiful flower arrangement waiting for my arrival. It was from my friend, Heidi, and it touched me that she'd remembered and thought to show her caring in this way. She also invited me to her home that day.

I immediately emailed her a note of thanks along with my confession that I couldn't be alone and would come to her place later that evening.

I was so tired.

First I had to rest.

Then I would go see Heidi and Pete, my friends.

Once I'd sent my email I noticed one sent to me from my son's best friend, Corey, and his wife, Kirsten. They just wanted to let me know they were thinking of me on this sad day.

I shared part of the day with people that cared about my son, too. That was my desire and they made it come true. Their words touched my heart and made me cry.

The tears don't soothe.

They just come.

Today I feel angry.

I don't know where to direct my anger.

I'm angry at the world that takes for granted having their children when I don't have mine.

It's an unfair anger, but nothing much is fair right now.

Day 142

"Two men looked out from prison bars,
One saw mud, the other saw stars"

It is an old saying I picked up somewhere and have never forgotten. I've even been known to quote it quite often in hopes of encouraging a despondent friend who couldn't see the positive in a negative situation.

I know it is all a person's attitude as to how one copes in everyday life. From my perspective and observations, it would appear those that whine the most get the least true problems. They worry, fret and fuss, and yet little happens to them.

My son never whined. He never complained. He was quiet in nature, or so I thought. It would now only appear he held everything in.

I understand.

I understood before but now I wholly understand.

I keep quiet now for I have nothing to say.

I feel angry now but have nowhere to vent.

I hold pain in for it knows no bounds should it ever escape.

I appear quiet in nature, but really, my soul is shattered and my heart, broken.

I'm not quiet in nature.

I'm just broken beyond repair.

Was this how my son felt?

I think it was.

I also think I knew.

I just didn't know how to help or what to do.

I'm sure people feel like that with me now.

The worst thing they can do is back away from me.

And yet that is exactly what I did with my son.

"I didn't know," seems like a silly excuse.

It's one we all use to make ourselves feel justified.

I should have known how bad it was.

I just didn't know how to help or what to do.

I still don't.

My next door neighbors in the complex, Betty and Val, have adopted a Mexican street dog and will be taking it back to Canada when they leave. The dog's name is Florecer, which means "flower" and this flower is anything but tame. Florecer is forever bouncing, barking, biting and quite entertaining to watch from afar.

Today, my quiet, well behaved perro, Kelly, and I had the pleasure of watching over Florecer while her owners went for dinner. As they were leaving, I was informed "Flower" needed to be let off the leash to do her business and was reassured she wouldn't run away.

Apparently, she was not given the same instructions, for immediately upon the leash being released, Florecer, the wild Mexican dog, took off like a shot and ran through the busy streets of La Penita, intent on finding her owners, with Kelly and me in hot pursuit.

What a chase through the town it was. Thoughts ran willy nilly through my mind as I chased one perro, hoping mine was still behind me, and wondered how I would explain to Betty and Val their dog was lost, or worse yet, run over.

She'd only been in my care for five minutes.

Exhausted, sweating, panting from exertion, Kelly and I spotted "Flower" up the road and it appeared she had caught up to her owners as they were about to catch a taxi ride to their dinner destination.

The dog was saved.

Grabbing both dogs, one on the leash, one not, I crossed the street only to almost get run over by a backing up truck. He was not watching behind him as is common here in Mexico, and it is up to the pedestrian to watch out for vehicles, for they stop where they please, go where they please, and even will make another lane where there is none to be had, thereby cutting off unsuspecting tourists out for a leisurely stroll.

It was time for me and the two perros to call it a night.

It was a diversion, albeit an almost disastrous one, but a diversion nonetheless.

Day 143

A year ago today I didn't know my son was already dead.

A year ago today I was in Arizona, laughing and laying by the pool with my friends.

A year ago today my biggest problem was no problem at all.

A year ago tomorrow my world shattered.

A year ago tomorrow I became the walking dead.

A year ago tomorrow I became a mother who would bury her only child.

A year ago tomorrow I prayed to die.

I continue to pray to die.

I cannot breathe.

My heart continues to beat but I feel no life within me.

My purpose in life is gone.

This was intended to be a book honoring my son and immortalizing his life.

Instead it is a book about my pain.

My pain and sorrows are too enormous to be ignored,

And have swallowed me up to where I now cease to exist as I was,

And never will be that person again.

A year ago today I was happy...

Day 144

A year ago today, March 25th, is when I heard the news my son was gone. In all fairness to this book, I should write the details, but maybe another day.

I can't bear this pain. I want to run away. I don't want to cry. I want things to be as I thought they were a year and one day ago.

I want my son to be alive.

Day 145

Today's lesson, boys and girls, is how I got ripped off by Jesus. No, not the biblical Jesus of days gone by, but Jesus (pronounced Haysus) the Mexican taxi driver in La Penita, Mexico.

Yesterday, I didn't know what to do, how to be, or where I fit on the first anniversary of the day I heard my son was dead. This is inconceivable. These words, these thoughts, these feelings; how is it I'm to function in a day?

Waking up tired, lethargic, and not wanting to do much of anything, I bought a kite and a blue rose I was somehow going to incorporate into commemorating the day. After breakfast, I decided Kelly and I would just go to the local beach here, fly the kite and throw the blue rose into the ocean.

I didn't want to cry.

My tears don't help and only hurt more.

I didn't want to cry.

Walking down the avenida towards the beach, I passed the taxi drivers and stopped to ask how much a collectivo, which is a large van and supposedly much cheaper than a taxi, would charge to take me and Kelly to Los de Marcos, a town about half an hour south of here, towards Puerto Vallarta. "One hundred and fifty pesos," I was told.

"Too much," I said, and proceeded on my way down the avenida.

The collectivo driver ran after me and said, "For you, senora, special today, one hundred and twenty pesos."

"The most I would pay is one hundred pesos," I retort.

"Ok, senora, you drive a hard bargain."

What was I doing?

I wasn't prepared.

I had no intention of going to Los de Marcos.

Off we went.

Sitting in the collectivo, amidst a flurry of other Mexican people, I started to cry.

The tears ran unabated, and would not stop, try as I must.

For some strange reason, I needed someone to know why I was crying and so told the collectivo driver I had lost my son a year ago and today I was going to a town I'd never been to remember him.

The taxi driver was very kind, told me his name was Jesus, and when he dropped off everyone else, would take me to the beach and spend some time with me.

He asked if I was all alone here in Mexico and I told him I was, except for my wonderful dog left to me by my son.

I thought I might die. I thought I was a silly woman for telling a stranger I was all alone here in Mexico and no one knew where I was. His persistence in spending alone time with me made me all the more wary.

It did not make me afraid, for I cared not for my life. My only concern was for Kelly the dog and I prayed to a God I no longer liked to protect her.

Stopping at the beach, I asked Jesus to help me put together my kite and he informed me a part of it was missing. Whittling out a piece of wood, he put it where the missing piece should have been.

Then, Jesus with the silver teeth and wizened brow, gave me a hug. He told me I was not alone in La Penita for now I had a friend in him. I paid him my one hundred pesos and proceeded on my way down the beach.

I flew my kite, cried for my son, and watched the angry ocean waves. They were gargantuan in size and beat against the ocean shore. My anger matched the ocean waves and I screamed and screamed and screamed.

I needed to see if the screaming inside me would feel better once it was allowed out, but felt no better for having done so.

Kelly and I walked the length of the beach in Los de Marcos and when we arrived at the rock bluffs, I threw the blue rose into the ocean and cried for my son. The ocean waves hit the rose and tore each petal from its stem. All that was left was the stem making its way towards shore.

The ocean waves matched my anger that day.

Catching the collectivo back home to La Penita, the driver charged me forty pesos, a fraction of what Jesus charged.

I was ripped off by Jesus.

At least he hugged me first...

Day 146

I don't feel well today. I never feel well emotionally, but today I physically feel ill again. My body is tired, enervated, without any vigor or force. It's all so tiring I can't even seem to muster up the energy to explain how I feel.

I feel sad.

I don't know what direction today's writing will go, for I am writing this chapter more out of a sense of duty to finish this book rather than a desire to write or a need to unravel the jumble my thoughts and emotions are in.. Usually, in my writing, I come to understand my feelings. Right now my feelings are so painful, I don't honestly know if I want to understand them, and maybe they should lie in a heap at the bottom of my heart, not being unraveled or understood.

Or not.

I don't know.

Nothing is very important to me anymore so I don't know from moment to moment what I want.

I want to write about Brad but the timid attempt at a relationship with him blew up in my face and now I'm feeling it was yet another loss.

Logically I understand we were not meant to be more than friends, but think I needed somewhere where I was the favorite; where I was the one someone couldn't wait to see, hold, kiss, touch, and think of a future with.

Now that I don't have that in him and we have gone back to a nice, comfortable, safe friendship, I feel the loss.

He is here right now and we had the discussion about why getting the email breaking up with me, almost as an afterthought, upset me so much. He was kind and nice because he is a kind, nice guy, but bottom line, he is free to pursue love and life and fun and women and adventure, while I'm tied up in this little box of pain. I told him how it terrified me when he got off the plane last time he came to visit because I knew my emotions had changed from friendship to the possibility of love, and he said he sensed a change in me, which made him back away more. We both agree that what happens in the spiritual, not physical realm is more real than what the eye can see. It reminds me of a saying I once heard, "Who you are is speaking so loud, I can't hear what you're saying."

At the time I was engrossed in the conversation and not wanting to get too emotional so it didn't occur to me until today to wonder what it was he sensed in me. I knew I had changed, become fearful, hopeful, desiring the object of my affection to return the feeling, but I said none of that. I acted as I always do. What was it he could sense? I don't know if I want to have another heavy conversation, so may ask him or may not.

It still hurts that I am alone in this world.

Thinking more on how we sense feelings made me wonder about my son and if he sensed my fear he would someday take his life. I saw him live through unimaginable horror as a child and tormented myself with what must be going on inside him to have lived through that.

When he looked, acted and behaved as though all was right in his world, even though I still had the niggling fear inside that it wasn't, I turned a blind eye, and pretended he was fine.

I didn't know what to do, so I did nothing.

Will I ever be able to forgive myself?

Somehow I need to for it is tearing me apart. It is eating away my soul, my spirit, my body, my mind.

I have to find a way.

But don't even have the energy to begin to try.

Day 147

I'm really upset today.

I had a dream my son was still alive and the dream was more real than my reality, for now I walk around in a constant daze, unable to remember conversations, people, or the simplest of tasks.

In the dream my son was in the hospital and had suffered major injuries which required surgery and stitches. When I arrived, he was awake and lucid, but it was obvious he was in a lot of pain.

I wanted to help, but didn't know how, so instead hugged him and we talked as we hadn't in a long time. While he was alive and still on earth, I knew, many times, he wanted to talk deeper with me. I was so afraid to face the pain of his childhood and so afraid he might want to talk about those events and circumstances that I kept the conversation light and laughed when I should have listened.

My son eventually gave up trying to talk to me about anything other than trivial things. I failed him.

Back to my dream.

A student nurse came in to check on the sutures and I quietly left the room, so thankful my son was alive, was going to get better, and this year following the funeral was just a nightmare we all were soon to wake up from.

Making my way back to his hospital room, my son writhed in agony, for this student nurse had accidentally cut one of his main arteries. "He might not make it," I heard the doctor say.

"No!" I screamed, for I had just got my son back. He couldn't leave again! He had to stay alive!

Rushing to his side, I saw the pain in his eyes. I also saw the kind, gentle, loving person he was inside.

He just couldn't die again.

My cousin had arrived from Ottawa and was anxiously pacing in the hospital waiting room. When I came out of my son's room, I asked my cousin who had we buried if my son was here, still alive?

She looked at me with sorrow in her eyes, while I waited for an answer to my question; an answer that would not come.

I was so filled with hope in my dream, and wanted us to win in life. I wanted my son and I to have a second chance and have a life of happiness and joy.

Then, I woke up.

And knew it was all just a dream.

I had buried my son that day.

I want to go back to sleep so I can dream about a son who is alive. I don't want to be awake on this earth, and know my son is not.

Day 148

Another sleepless night. What am I to do? The sadness wraps itself around me like a shroud and the lack of sleep makes it all the more unbearable.

My life is now broken beyond repair. The best I can hope for is to limp along, semi-dead, semi-alive, not belonging to this world or the one beyond, and wait. Wait, wait, wait; to go and be with my son.

Before he died, my life ambition was to have a life ambition. Only knowing me through the pages of this book, a reader would have no way of understanding how desperately I clung on to hope for a better life, how hard I fought, struggled and believed we would not only survive, but overcome.

We did neither, and the sense of being shackled by my circumstances and grief makes this existence unbearable.

I am only happy when I'm asleep and dreaming my son is still alive.

I reach out and search for happiness in so many other ways, but all to no avail.

Maybe my need is too great, maybe my pain is too prominent, maybe my desire to belong somewhere was never meant to be. Maybe I deserve the life I got.

Maybe I never should have believed for better.

I had to.

While my son was alive, I had to.

Now, I no longer do.

I'm too tired and exhausted to write anymore today.

Day 149

It's a cloudy day today and I'm not sure what to say. I woke up early with the achy, sniffly, sore throat, fever kind of feeling. I'm usually quite low energy but even more so now with being sick so much.

The illness robs me of the smidgeon of coping mechanisms I have and shoots me lower than low. I can't seem to find any reprieve from the sorrow when I'm also battling my body while it is battling me.

It would be fine if I died. It would stop this continual pain. When I feel like this, I understand how my son must have felt, and it rips the very core of my being to know my baby was in that amount of pain.

Could I have helped more?

Yes, I could have.

Could I have stopped the wheels in motion?

I like to think I could have.

Could I have protected him more in life?

I definitely could have.

I just wanted us to be loved.

And since I couldn't change the rest of the world to make them love us, I changed us to make us lovable and beyond reproach.

The sick, sad feeling this gives me has no reprieve.

While many say time will heal, I will live and love again, I know I won't.

I know I will carry the burden of what my child suffered for the rest of my days.

Can anyone fault me for wanting the rest of my days to be short?

Day 150

I'm sick again. Weak and sick and tired.
Don't know what else to say,
So, won't say anything more.

Day 151

What's there to say?
My son is dead.
Who cares about anything else?

Day 152

God, I feel so alone.

I feel so confused and shattered and frightened and don't understand how I ended up so alone and unloved.

Or am I loved, but just don't know it?

I was loved by my son and pushed him away.

I did to him what was done to me, where nothing I did was ever good enough, nothing I said was ever smart enough, nothing I thought was ever acceptable enough.

I was raised in a family where I was definitely the scapegoat for their bad moods. Wanting to please and wanting to be loved, I let them verbally mistreat me and aimed higher and higher to become "People Pleaser of the World."

I succeeded, but it still wasn't good enough.

I still fell short in their eyes, and when they were done with me, they started on my son. Before my son was even three days old, my older brother said my baby was demon possessed and needed an exorcism. My mentally insane mother quickly agreed and an exorcism was set in place for my baby's first Christmas on this earth, when he was only ten days old.

It only went downhill from there and the kinder he tried to be, the crueler they became. Since they were the only family we had, and I so desperately wanted family for my little boy, I put up with this sick, twisted family and their shenanigans and tried to make my son and I good enough, or lovable enough.

One day my son said to me, "Mom, you try so hard to please your brothers and others in this family. Have you ever thought they aren't worth it?"

No, son, I hadn't. I thought we weren't good enough and needed to be better. I'm sorry, son.

I wish I could change even now, but no longer know how.

I don't know how to stop trying to please others, and don't know how to stop trying to be loved, even in my grief.

Or maybe it's my grief that makes me now so afraid to face the rest of my life alone, and I so desperately want someone there to share my pain and hold me while I cry.

I don't know what I want to do.

I don't know how to cope day by day.

I don't know how to cope minute by minute.

I no longer know how to be.

I am so sad.

And I just want someone to be there.

Maybe I want too much...

Day 153

I don't want to write today either. How many times have I said that in this journal, and yet I continue to plod along, hoping something I write, think or feel will somehow lighten the pain, lighten the load, make me feel there is a purpose, small though it may be, to my life?

Brad and his daughter left today and I always feel sad when he leaves me. It is a difficult place to be when you are attached to a person that maybe, quite possibly, is not as attached to you.

I lean on him for my grief. I don't know why him and not somebody else. It's just how it turned out and now, while he continues leading a normal life, I am constantly afraid I will do or say something that will make him leave my life and then I won't have the shoulder I so desperately need to lean on.

How is it I have nowhere to be totally free in my grief and feel a freedom to vent, kick, scream, yell, cry, cry, cry? How is it I feel trapped behind a plastic mask trying to put on a brave front because if I don't, there may not be anyone there to care?

As it is, I sometimes feel the relationships I have are shaky ones and fear they can leave me much easier than I can leave them. My fears have not come out of thin air. They have come from years of being pushed aside, tossed aside, and treated as though slightly inferior.

Eleanor Roosevelt said, "No one can make you feel inferior without your permission," and I've never forgotten that quote. I give my permission too often, but after so many years of being that way, now don't know how to change.

Apparently, while Brad was preparing for his trip here, I was supposed to arrange a shuttle to pick him and the girls up. His plans were very vague and he sent an email telling me not to worry about a shuttle, so I gave him the phone number to the shuttle service and thought my work there was done. Normally, I'm someone who bends over backwards to help and ends up doing things people don't even ask for, but he reassured he had the matter looked after.

Since Brad and I have been on shaky ground as we are trying to figure out this friendship we have, I've tried to be as genial as possible and have waited for him to show the next step in our friendship. I have no gauge when it comes to people, and don't even know if what I say makes sense, or what I do is acceptable to their boundaries or not.

For you see I no longer have any boundaries. What would anything possibly matter to me now? You say I matter? Not in my mind, I don't.

It appeared the week with Brad was going fairly well until two nights before he left. We were sitting on my deck and he brought up how upset he was that I couldn't do a simple thing like get a shuttle for him. I was shocked and for a moment, couldn't respond. The more I tried to explain, the angrier he got. The angrier he got, the more attacked I felt. Soon we were yelling at each other over silly, nonsensical things and I wondered how this had happened.

I wondered, how, with what I am going through and with how very difficult it is for me to even function, that someone could get angry over a misunderstanding as trivial as this.

And yet, he has been so kind to me in so many ways. He has been the strong support I sometimes cling to when I can't rise above the pain.

I have no gauge.

I think the anger was over more than a shuttle ride.

I don't know what to do.

He is my constant.

And all I know to do when attacked is run.

I've already started to back away and run, but don't even know if that is what he wants.

We're just people, trying to find our way.

My way didn't work.

My son is gone.

Day 154

I'm afraid to go home. I'm so incredibly petrified and terrified to go home.

Two weeks today I leave Mexico and while it hasn't been a winter vacation where I have basked and frolicked in the sand and surf, it still has somehow been less frightening than the prospect of going home.

I need to go home.

I think.

What else am I supposed to do?

Where else can I go?

Running away to Mexico has not worked to numb the sadness and I can't ever imagine a life without this pain. I don't know what I had hoped to achieve by my Mexican misadventure but knew I couldn't stay home. Now, I am afraid to return.

For you see, I have no one waiting for me there.

I have no one missing me and saying they can't wait for me to get home.

I will have no arms to hug me when I get there.

I won't have a son to call to tell him of my journey.

I will have four empty walls and a shroud of silence to greet me.

I will have my son's grave only two blocks from where I live.

I will have the headstone I still have to purchase for him.

I will have the memory of no new memory of him for this year.

I will have the loneliness, the emptiness, the fear, and the grief.

I will have supporters that have moved on for it has now been almost a year since his funeral.

I will have the pity.

I will feel the despair.

I will have the life I lived without the most important facet of my existence.

I will have the pictures sitting in a box in his empty bedroom.

I will have the grief; the grief that never sleeps; the grief that never lets me sleep.

I will have the never ending tears.

I am afraid to go home and am resisting the passing of the moments with every ounce of my strength, with every breath of my being.

I cannot stop time.

I cannot undo the past.

I cannot change the saddest day of my life.

I cannot bear to live without my son.

I am afraid to go home...

Day 155

If I had written earlier in the day, this would have been a sad chapter, full of tears and self-recrimination, as I was tired and mournful.

Tonight I had plans with Heidi and Pete to go for dinner and they invited a few of their friends. All day long, whilst dragging my sorry butt on the broken cobblestone pavement that is my street of Cristobal Calle, I didn't want to go.

I didn't want to interact with people and maybe, possibly, probably make anyone unhappy with anything I said, did, or thought. It appears I attract irascible people to me and bring out the worst in them.

I can't deal with anyone else's dissatisfaction of how I act, react, or basically zone out from the comings and goings of the human race.

Please, people, be gentler with me.

I am doing the best I can.

Some of you are.

And to you I say thank you.

You know who you are.

It was my responsibility to organize the restaurant and I had been talking about the spareribs so much that Pete was mentally tasting them and salivating doing so.

To this restaurant we would go tonight, along with their friends, whose company I also greatly enjoyed.

The restaurant was closed.

Everyone was hungry.

I felt responsible, for it was up to me.

I can't keep up, people.

I barely match my socks.

Why can't I make people understand?

Probably because I didn't understand.

I've been where you are at; you just haven't been where I'm at.

We ended up at a Teriyaki restaurant, had a wonderful meal with excellent conversation, and everyone was home by 8 p.m.

It was another day passed by.

When I'm with people, I sometimes forget for a moment.

Now, I'm alone and I remember.

I am still afraid to go home.

I think I am more afraid to be alone there.

Day 156

I always think, throughout the day, about what I'm going to write and then, when I sit down and put proverbial pen to paper, my best laid plans sometimes go by the wayside.

Sometimes they don't.

I was initially thinking to write about Kelly the dog and see what unfolded.

Many times throughout the week we walk the same pathway to the beach in Rincon de Guayabitos. We begin from home, as I've come to know our little apartment, and walk down the avenida to the ice cream store where we turn left and proceed on our way until we come to a swinging suspension bridge.

Once we cross the bridge, we are in the town of Rincon de Guayabitos in the subdivision appropriately dubbed Gringo Gulch, for it is where all the whiteys have built their mega mansions. The contrast between La Penita and Guayabitos is as night and day; one side poor and mostly Mexican, the other side wealthy and mostly Anglo Saxon.

Kelly and I walk Gringo Gulch until we turn down a pathway leading us to a bridge that brings us to the ocean where I throw a stick into the water for Kelly and she never seems to tire of chasing it.

So far, there is nothing particularly newsworthy about my story.

What is interesting is that Kelly my dog has gotten to know where other dogs reside and which bark the loudest.

Even though she is a formidable looking pit bull cross, she is a big chicken; a lovable big chicken, but a chicken nonetheless.

At first I didn't understand when, during our brisk walk, Kelly would suddenly stop dead in her tracks and refuse to move any further. I would tug at her leash almost to the point of her fairly tight collar sliding off her head. Still she would refuse to go further with me.

Sometimes when it was very hot and I would be perspiring profusely, intent on reaching my final destination, I would get annoyed with Kelly and cajole, coax and try to maneuver her, all to no avail.

Kelly was afraid of the barking dogs, even the ones safely locked behind the huge iron gates. She would not move.

Understanding finally dawned in a light bulb moment and I felt sorry for Kelly, for, I, too, am afraid of anyone barking at me. I feel I would shatter into a million pieces if anyone looked at me sideways, and I'm nowhere near as formidable looking as Kelly.

What to do with my loving perro?

I have now begun to learn where all the barking dogs are, too. When we come close to them, and Kelly screeches to a grinding halt, I tell her it's ok and we cross the road to walk on the other sidewalk.

She readily agrees and walks along until we come to the next house with a barking dog.

Then, we cross the street again.

Sometimes there are barking dogs on both sides of the street and then we walk in the middle of the road, careful not to get run over by a motorist.

Anyone watching would think I am drunk, zigging and zagging along the cobblestone roads.

I am merely being kind.

While it may look funny, it really is such a minor inconvenience to me.

But to Kelly, it makes her fears a little less tangible.

I wanted to tell my son this story.

He would have found it amusing and been happy at how well I am looking after his dog.

I cried today when I realized my son would never hear this story.

I cried on the street in the midst of dodging barking dogs...

Day 157

Do you ever have one of those nightmares that are real? You know the ones where there is some deep, dark disaster looming or possibly happening and you are so sure your sleeping state is one of wakefulness. In your dream, you may moan, you may cry out, you may awaken startled, disconcerted or overwrought, but awaken you do.

Remember the relief you feel when the realization comes that it was only a nightmare; it was only a dream. It was not your reality and your reality is safe and exactly as it should be.

For a moment you lay there, reveling in the contentment and security that comes with knowing you had only been sleeping; you had only been dreaming. Your world is still safe and the loved ones you may have dreamt were injured or worse are still alive and well.

My nightmare is the opposite.

While I sleep, I dream we were triumphant and were living the life we had overcome many obstacles to obtain.

When I awake, I hope I am still dreaming, for my reality is unbearable.

I can't write anymore today.

My dying spirit is overcome with sorrow and the suffering I am enduring is too painful to describe.

I will write more tomorrow.

Day 158

This insomnia is driving me crazy. I take sleeping pills, sleep aids, fall asleep fine and then am awake after a few hours.

All day long I'm groggy and lethargic and the world looks even darker than it was before. When I hear someone laughing, it sounds sharp and edgy and I wish they would stop.

No sleep is making an already unhappy person even unhappier.

Today I couldn't find a place for myself. My conversation is stilted and it is an arduous task putting one word in front of the other in an attempt to make a sentence.

I have lots to say.

I just don't want to write anymore.

Am I winding down?

Or am I that afraid to go home and see the fruitlessness of writing my journal?

I don't know.

I guess I don't really care.

I am undone.

Day 159

You would think with only a week left here in Mexico and subsequently only a week left of writing this book, I would have something profound to say.

You would think my last few chapters would be full of witty repertoire and deep, heartfelt emotions.

You would think.

Instead I find myself feeling like a deflating balloon. I find the fear that surrounds me is all the more paramount as my departure date looms, for my departure date from Mexico parallels my arrival date in Canada and the home I now detest the sight of.

I don't want to go home.

I don't really care to stay in Mexico.

I don't know where I want to go, other than to leave this earth.

I am afraid of the future to be faced without my son.

I am afraid to be as alone as I feel.

I am just afraid.

Someone suggested I just give in to the fear for what do I have to lose now? If I lose my mind, so what? If I fall apart, so what?

The "so what" that fills me with trepidation is should any of the above mentioned events occur, there will be nobody there to pick me up.

I fear I will lie wherever I fall.

My neighbor here in Mexico, who was a schoolteacher, told me a student she was very close to was killed in a car accident. My neighbor was very traumatized by the untimely death of this sixteen year old who had so much potential and such a bright future ahead of her.

This neighbor kept it together and seemed to be handling her grief well, until one day she walked into the office and just fell apart. She fell apart and could not get control of her emotions and basically had to be helped to get better. She said it just hit her without warning for the grief was bottled up and needed to come out.

When I'm in public and the grief hits, I groan. It is a quiet, close lipped groan I can feel emanate from somewhere so deep inside me I never knew of its existence until this terrible tragedy occurred. The groan sounds like a wounded animal and I quickly control the decibel level for fear someone will hear me. If someone does turn towards me, I quickly cough, in hopes of covering the unnatural, guttural sound my soul has just made.

When I'm alone, I feel the silent scream inside me saying, "No, no, no, please, no." I am beseeching God or the universe to make the reality of my son's death a supposition based on no solid foundation, and am hoping, praying, crying out to the god's, to make it not so.

The silent scream goes on in my sleep; it goes on in my waking hours. It is a grieving mother praying she no longer has a reason to grieve.

What if my groan escapes the restraints I've put around it?

What if my silent scream becomes vociferous and I can't stop it?

Who will I become?

What will I become?

Will anyone care?

Day 160

Today I feel angry. I feel angry that no matter what I now do in the future to better my life, my son does not have the same chance. No matter what fame or fortune may come my way, my son will still be gone.

I feel angry for all the people who are still alive that weren't as good as my son. While you may say everyone deserves to live, and I agree, some so desperately want to leave this world and live their lives only to cause misery to others.

My son was a gentle, kind soul who deserved so much more than he got in life. He deserved a family who loved him, instead of one that was cruel.

He deserved a mother who didn't have to struggle as hard as I struggled just to survive. He deserved to come home from school to freshly baked cookies instead of a lonely apartment in a lonely city.

I knew there was so much lacking in our lives, but thought if I could just pretend everything was fine, then fine it would be. I thought, if I could just fool him into thinking we were making out alright, then maybe I could fool myself just a little.

My son and I, we played the game.

We played the game of I'm fine if you're fine. Are you sure you're fine? Please don't tell me you're not because then I may have to break down and tell you I'm not. Let's just pretend instead.

The only one truly pretending was me.

He tried to be real.

He tried to talk to me about all the horrendous things that went on in our lives.

He tried to understand a life no child should have to live through.

I was so afraid of what happened happening that I couldn't bear to let him know how alone we really were.

I pretended.

I pretended we were loved and cared about and belonged somewhere in this world.

That's all it was; a pretense. For no one cared and when we were abused, no one wanted to help. They just wanted us to go away so our pain wouldn't make their lives uncomfortable. They wanted us to go away so the person afflicting us wouldn't turn and notice them.

So, we went away.

And we stopped asking for help.

And we stopped believing or hoping anyone would ever be there to care.

And when we stopped, we were told we should have tried harder.

We should have let ourselves be rejected and rejected and still worked harder to make people love us.

We shouldn't have given up.

We didn't know what else to do.

I still hung onto a small glimmer of hope my son would be compensated as an adult for the painful existence he had to endure as a child.

That hope was all that kept me going.

Now, it no longer exists for he no longer exists.

Now, I can give myself permission to give up.

I think I already have...

Day 161

I'm so afraid to go home I can barely function. Not that I functioned so well before, but as my departure date from Mexico is rapidly advancing, I feel almost mesmerized by the fear.

I'm afraid to go home.

Look what happened the last time I went home.

While logically I know the same thing can't happen again, I now function more from instinct than logic and so my instincts are deceiving me into thinking everyone else of importance in my life is now gone, too.

I'm bracing myself.

I'm preparing myself for more bad news.

I'm sure there is disaster upon disaster awaiting me.

I am as someone returning from a war.

I am shell shocked.

I can feel something is wrong inside me and I am fighting so hard to hold on.

I freeze when there is any confrontation coming my way.

I freeze and don't unthaw until hours later.

When I unthaw, I am angry.

Today I am angry.

I am angry at all the trivial, nonsensical, imbecile things people want me to still be able to do.

I am angry my son is gone.

I am angry I stayed behind.

I am just angry.

But, more than that,

I am defeated...

Day 162

Today was just a weird day. Kelly got snapped at twice by two dogs half her size, and she just stood there and took it. She reminded me of us, my son and me. We just stood there and took it, until one of us couldn't take it anymore.

Now, the other lives with the regrets of all the times she should have spoken up and didn't. She will live with those regrets forever.

Today I looked after the neighbor's dog, Flores, and the three of us went walking down the avenida of La Penita until we came to the suspension bridge that would take us over to Guayabitos. At the beach in Guayabitos, the dogs played and frolicked in the water. Flores, being livelier and younger, was behaving like a Mexican street dog, as the ever patient Kelly stood idly by. It was how my son behaved. He never made waves, never caused a ruckus, never made anyone feel inconvenienced in any way.

I taught him that, for I behaved in the same way.

Now, it seems too much of an effort to behave any other way.

I can see myself becoming a total recluse.

I can see myself hiding away from people and hiding away from the harsh reality that is this world.

Or my perception of this world.

Some may see it as beautiful.

I saw it as beautiful.

I was wrong.

Now, I wonder what the next person is going to say to hurt me.

Now, I wonder how much I will have to suck it up and hold in my feelings while others think they know what to tell me to do.

If there is kindness in this world, other than a few, I don't see it.

I see it as cruel.

I am afraid to live in this world for I don't know how.

I'm not doing a very good job of it.

For my son is gone.

I thought the ending of this book would bring some light, some hope, some easing from the pain.

It brought none of those things and I feel this sorrow is my destiny. My choice, I know. You don't have to tell me.

And you don't have a right to judge me until you feel what I'm feeling.

No one has a right to tell someone else how to feel.

I hate all the people who tried to do exactly that.

I probably hate myself, too.

I think my fear of going home to nothing has overshadowed so many other emotions.

Day 163

Last night I awoke at two a.m. only to see a large cockroach climbing my bedroom ceiling. At the time I wasn't sure it was a cockroach and it didn't bother me much, so I continued to watch it as it slowly made its way across the room.

What bothered me more was that I was awake and upset at two a.m. and sleep evaded me.

Finally, tired of watching the meanderings of the cockroach, I opened my balcony door and grabbed my walking stick to try and shoo this recalcitrant creature out my door.

Who knew cockroaches could fly?

It dove straight for me, I let out a shriek that could have woken the city block, and ran for cover.

The cockroach flew into my kitchen area and is yet to be found.

I think it's time to leave Mexico.

I just don't want to go home.

Since the weather has warmed up these past few weeks, my apartment has been besieged by tiny ants and they appear to be everywhere. Upon first sighting, I felt quite repugnant, but as time has gone by, now I merely swipe them away with my hand, and if they land in the cooking salt I have beside the two burner hot plate, I pick them out and throw them away.

We acclimate or we crumble; our choice.

I'm really not sure what to do here anymore in Mexico and found the day long and boring. The sun is too hot to spend much time sun tanning and I have made so few friends here, there is no one I can just go and visit.

Yesterday we walked the beach in Guayabitos which is something Kelly and I both enjoy, but the water has now been assailed by stinging jellyfish and we saw many on the shore. It is a deterrent for walking the beach and, as we only have four days left here, yesterday was probably the last day for beach walking and tossing the stick for my perro.

Is it Mexico or is it me?

Last year when I was in Tucson, Arizona, there were many things that went wrong and the weather was the worst they had for many years. I still had a marvelous time in Arizona and to this day, say it was my best winter ever, until I heard the news of my son.

So, is it Mexico or is it me?

In an attempt to cheer myself up, I went to the hairdresser to get beautified. This is the same hairdresser I've had since coming to La Penita almost six months ago, and if this were Canada, we would know each other's life stories by now. As this is Mexico and she speaks no English, we converse mostly in hand gestures and my miniscule knowledge of Spanish. Still she recognizes me and Kelly when we come in, and she remembers Kelly's name.

Today she asked if I had an esposo, which is Spanish for husband. I said no and then told her I also had lost my son. I knew enough Spanish to say those words and when uttered, the tears ran down my cheeks.

The hairdresser asked about other immediate family and I said I had nobody, to which she looked at my dog and said, "Solo Kelly," which means "only Kelly." I said "Si". (yes)

Her look of pity made me want to leap out of my chair and run. I could see longer strands of hair where she'd forgotten to cut them and normally would have asked that she cut them, but this time said nothing.

"Just let me out of here", I thought.

I can't bear anyone's pity.

I can't bear the truth that I have no one now that my son is gone.

I can't bear this was my greatest fear, and now it is realized.

I paid her quickly and ran out of there, no longer able to control the tears.

With each step I took, I heard the words in my mind replay themselves. "You must deserve this or it wouldn't have happened. You must deserve this pain."

How do you stop those thoughts?

I wanted this book to end on a positive note; if not for you, then for me.

I hate that my sorrow is no better now than when I started writing.

I hate there is nowhere to escape this pain.

I hate that I can't sleep through a night.

I hate that my radar is askew and I no longer have a concept of right or wrong.

My world has shattered and everything is upside down.

So, is it Mexico or is it me?

It is so definitely me...

Day 164

Today was a different day. After spending quite a few on my own with just Kelly the dog, I had plans to meet Babs for lunch to say goodbye.

We sat at a restaurant on the beach and drank a few beers with our lunch. Conversation flowed easily and two hours passed quickly by.

Leaving her amongst promises to keep in touch and accolades of what wonderful people we were, my step home was a bit lighter than it's been for a while.

I realized something.

I realized pain is much more painful when alone.

I realized grief is much more grievous when alone.

I realized my greatest fear of going home is being alone.

But, how do you make someone love you?

How do you make people want to be with you?

I have spent my entire life playing the part of a chameleon that changes at will to suit you and your mood.

It didn't work.

I still feel so alone.

I want to break down and truly feel my grief.

I want to cry and scream if I need to.

I want someone to be there, and don't want to be alone.

I don't know who would agree to be there with me.

This isn't how I intended this chapter to go, but then the chapters rarely go as I intended.

Coming back from my very socially successful lunch, I felt tired and laid down for a nap. For the first time in a long time I awoke refreshed. My day had been happy so my sleep had been too.

It's not rocket science.

No one needs a psychology degree to get it.

Feeling reasonably upbeat, I remembered my landlady had said she would take me to her doctor today to get some sleeping pills that worked very well for her.

Off we went.

The doctor spoke no English at all and it fell upon my landlady to translate. Her conversation with the doctor took a long time and she wouldn't stop to tell me what was being said. As I knew I was the topic of conversation, it irritated me to know I was being talked about and yet no one was translating.

A few times the doctor would look in my direction, say something, and the two of them would laugh. When I'd ask her what it was about, she would say one or two words, and finally told me the supposed sleeping pills I was taking from home were really antidepressants and were the type that would make me lively, upbeat, hyper, and wide awake.

I was shocked to hear this and would have thought I'd misunderstood the directions except the label on the bottle said to take three at night to help me sleep.

It was a confusing, frustrating time with this doctor and my landlady and no one was hearing, listening to, or understanding my questions. I walked out of there, prescription in hand, two hundred pesos poorer and feeling more helpless than when I went in.

Strange how now so many little things can dampen my spirit and make a reasonably happy day irritating.

I have to keep remembering this is Mexico and nothing is taken too seriously.

Before my son died, I would have fit right in...

Day 165

My time here in Mexico is coming to an end. In a way I feel slightly apprehensive finishing this book as it was a bit like visiting with an old friend; an old friend I felt comfortable enough with to say all I wanted or needed to say; an old friend who would listen without judgment and let me just be me; an old friend who knew I so desperately needed to talk more than I needed advice or words of wisdom to help me through this lamentable, cataclysmic time.

I will miss this old friend and I will miss the structured routine of feeling a need to sit and write my chapter a day. I now need some structure in my life and when I have none, do nothing.

What will I do now?

Start another book?

Continue to journal?

To what end?

I don't know if it has helped me profoundly or but for a moment. Maybe for the moment it did bring me comfort to pour out my pain, this book is worth it. Maybe it will be worth continuing to journal. I don't know.

I know, many days I didn't want to write and said so in my chapters. Now that I no longer have to, will I?

At this point, probably not.

For, while writing was cathartic, it was also restricting and I felt an obligation to write every day.

Now that those self-induced rules are no longer a part of me, I will feel a certain freedom not being bound by them.

I will also feel a certain loss.

I wanted this journal to bring about some deep

insight or understanding, originating in or penetrating to the depths of one's being, going far beyond what is superficial, external or obvious.

Did I succeed?

The more I think I know in life, the less I know.

So, I will leave Mexico, which has not been unkind to me. I have journeyed as far as I can journey here and now will move on.

What awaits me and Kelly the dog, I don't know.

I know I have no hope for a bright future, no thoughts for a better day, no certainty joy will fill me.

My son is gone.

What else can there possibly be?

Day 166

Tomorrow is April 17, 2011. Tomorrow is a year to the day I buried my son. I had a funeral and watched his casket lower into the ground, while onlookers watched me weep.

It was a day that never should have been.

Today I am packing to leave for tomorrow will be a sad day.

As is today...

Day 167

Today is one year to the day that I buried my son. His funeral date is April 17, 2010.

Tomorrow, Kelly the dog and I leave Mexico to fly home.

The next day, April 19th, is my birthday.

It will always be two days after the anniversary of the day I buried my son.

Happy Birthday to me...

90433680R00195

Made in the USA
Lexington, KY
11 June 2018